Benj. Franklin

John Adams

Hutchinson

W. Howe

Gen. Gage

Lord North

Samuel Adams's Revolution

SAMUEL ADAMS
(Portrait by John Singleton Copley)

CASS CANFIELD

Samuel Adams's Revolution

1765-1776

With the Assistance of George Washington,

Thomas Jefferson, Benjamin Franklin, John Adams,

George III, and the People of Boston

HARPER & ROW, PUBLISHERS

New York, Hagerstown, San Francisco, London

Credits for endpaper photographs: James Otis: Wichita Art Museum. George III and Lord North: National Portrait Gallery, London. John Hancock and John Adams: Museum of Fine Arts, Boston. Thomas Hutchinson: Massachusetts Historical Society. William Howe, Israel Putnam, Benedict Arnold and Thomas Gage: New York Public Library. Benjamin Franklin: Historical Society of Pennsylvania.

Designed by Dorothy Schmiderer

Maps by Harry Scott

Library of Congress Cataloging in Publication Data

Canfield, Cass.
  Samuel Adams's revolution. 1765–1776.

  Bibliography: p.
  Includes index.
    1. Adams, Samuel, 1722–1803. 2. United States—
History—Revolution, 1775–1783—Causes. I. Title.
E302.6.A2C36 1976   973.3'092'4   75–29937
ISBN 0–06–010619–0

76 77 78 79 10 9 8 7 6 5 4 3 2

Contents

Illustrations

Maps

Acknowledgments

I am grateful, first of all, to Joan H. King for her research on Sam Adams and on American women of the colonial period. She was also helpful in discovering illustrative material for this book.

To Richard B. Morris and John A. Garraty I am grateful for historical guidance. And I wish to thank Lynne McNabb for uncovering some facets of Sam Adams's career concerning which I had previously been unaware. To Richard E. Passmore I am once more indebted for constructive criticism; as well as to Simon Michael Bessie and to Mariana Fitzpatrick.

I also wish to acknowledge help from John Adams. His diaries and letters supplied me with much information about his second cousin, Sam. Without them it would have been difficult to accumulate details about Samuel Adams's life, for he kept few records. According to John, Sam burned them in the wintertime and tore them up in the summer. He feared to implicate his associates in revolutionary activities.

Among the books used in the preparation of *Sam Adams's Revolution* I found among the most useful: Allen French's *The Siege of Boston*, Arthur Tourtellot's *William Diamond's Drum*, John C. Miller's *Sam Adams: Pioneer in Propaganda* and Catherine Drinker Bowen's *The Miracle at Philadelphia*.

To my son, Michael

Author's Note

I was led to write this historical essay by my interest in an ancestor, Jonathan Cass, my great-great-grandfather, who served as a captain in the Revolution, fought in most of its battles from Bunker Hill to Yorktown—and attracted the favorable notice of General Washington. He was a tall, handsome man, with black, penetrating eyes, who came from New Hampshire.

I decided to investigate how Jonathan Cass and his compatriots lived and to learn more about the men who led the revolt against England. After some study it appeared that there was reason for a new look at the Revolution. Although no new facts were likely to emerge, it seemed as if fresh interpretations might be called for.

Samuel Adams proved to offer the basis for a fresh interpretation since, as I read about the period, it became clear that his role had not been fully appreciated. Of Sam, his second cousin, John Adams wrote in 1819: "A systematic course has been pursued for thirty years to run him down. His merits, and services and sufferings are beyond all calculation." In fact, it is apparent to me that it was primarily Adams who fanned the flame of rebellion and that he did so more effectively than any other major American leader. Without him, in my opinion, American independence could not have been declared in 1776.

Holding these views, I decided on the title "Samuel Adams's Revolution." Because my emphasis on Adams's place among Revolutionary leaders is greater than in most other accounts of the period, this book differs from others on the subject.

Foreword

The Tory governor of Massachusetts called him "the master of the puppets" and the King put a price on his head. Both paid grudging tribute to Samuel Adams, the stormy petrel of the American Revolution, to his incomparable gifts as an organizer of the masses and an instigator of subversive activities.

Indeed, considering Adams's principal role, he has been largely crowded out of the central cast of characters evoked by the commemoration of the Bicentennial of the American Revolution. In many respects a prototype of more recent revolutionaries—impecunious, discontented, unsurpassed in handling crowds and skillful at creating confrontation, Samuel Adams hardly fits the image of the elitist leaders whom we call the Founding Fathers.

In restoring Sam Adams to his central role as a tenacious and uncompromising leader of the independence movement, we are immensely indebted to Cass Canfield's book. With sympathy, insight and good humor the author recreates not only Sam Adams the Revolutionary, but the times in which he lived. Through these pages we see Adams's extraordinary rise as an agitator, mass organizer and political manipulator. Comparable to Thomas Paine as a master propagandist, Adams, as this book reveals, was far more sophisticated in employing the devices of mass demonstrations and economic boycotts, and far more innovative in creating an infrastructure that has served as a model for later revolutionary movements.

This book prudently ends with the initial battles on the eve of independence, for with Congress's formal Declaration of Independence, a moment of supreme triumph for Adams, that republican Puritan may well have realized that his major objective had been achieved and that the operation of the war itself and the winning of independence might best be left to the many talented men whom he, perhaps more than any other man, had drawn into the conflict. Men more gifted in the arts of statecraft, more creative, and indubitably more moderate and less inflexible would now take and keep the center of the stage.

But it was Samuel Adams's revolution, and Cass Canfield's engrossing book never lets us forget it for a moment.

RICHARD B. MORRIS

Samuel Adams's Revolution

I

Samuel Adams:
Born to Rebel

THE BRITISH GOVERNOR of Massachusetts, Francis Bernard, exclaimed about Sam Adams: "Every dip of his pen stung like a horned snake."[1] He was, indeed, a master of covert propaganda, which he directed against the injustices of British rule in the colonies.

Adams was a man of many parts. His ability to sway men's opinions and the use he made of his hatred of George III's despotic policies reveal the facets of a fascinating character. He lived at a time when American statesmen attained a stature never since equaled in our history.

The emergence of outstanding men in any given period is hard to explain, but in the colonies the spread of education, the challeng-

1. From "Firebrand of the Revolution" by Alexander Winston. *American Heritage,* April 1967.

ing economic opportunities, social mobility and training in self-government all created a favorable climate. George Washington, Samuel and John Adams, Franklin, Jefferson, Dr. Joseph Warren, to name a few, were all extraordinary men. Among the generals under Washington, Benedict Arnold, though he turned traitor, was outstanding, and military leaders like Nathanael Greene, Richard Montgomery and Ethan Allen were also first-rate.

In *The Spirit of 'Seventy-Six,* Henry Steele Commager and Richard B. Morris write:

> From the beginning to end the Revolution was led by an elite, not only benevolent and enlightened, but *prosperous and conservative*[2]—the leaders constituted perhaps the most conservative, respectable and disinterested revolutionary agitators that any revolution ever confessed. . . . They deprecated alike fanaticism and lawlessness and it is a curious commentary on the American temperament that the eloquent and devoted Tom Paine was distrusted almost as much as the odious Benedict Arnold.

Samuel Adams—not prosperous and conservative—was born over half a century before the Battle of Lexington, which marked the beginning of the Revolution, but by the time he had graduated from Harvard the protest against English rule had started. He attained maturity as his father was struggling against a Parliamentary order that threatened his financial ruin. "From his parents Adams inherited a strenuous Calvinism that was to make his vision of the conflict with Britain resemble a huge and murky illustration for *Paradise Lost.* . . . He saw England through a glass darkly: her government venal, her manners effeminate and corrupt, her religion Popish. In saving the colonies from her tyranny he believed that he also helped to save their manly virtues, and to make of Boston a 'Christian Sparta'—chaste, austere and godly."[3]

Samuel Adams's character did not fit into the general pattern of the Adams family; there seemed no room in that distinguished group

2. Italics added.
3. From "Firebrand of the Revolution," *op. cit.*

for a propagandist, democrat and backstairs politician.

There were two branches of the New England Adamses in the eighteenth century: between the town and country Adamses striking differences were evident. For the most part, the descendants of Henry Adams, founder of the family in rural New England, were obscure yeomen fifty years after the Boston Adamses had become prominent merchants and politicians. John Adams of rural Braintree (now Quincy, Massachusetts) ranked sixteenth in his Harvard class at a time when rank was determined by social position, while Sam of Boston had ranked sixth in his class of twenty-three a few years earlier (until lack of funds forced him to serve as a waiter in the college dining hall). Nevertheless, the country Adamses, from whom John was descended, had outstripped the Boston branch by the end of the Revolution.

Sam Adams, called Samuel by John Adams and probably by his friends, born September 16, 1722, was an infinitely complicated man, despite his plain Boston ancestry. His father, Deacon Samuel Adams, a pillar of the Congregational Church, was a "malsier" who owned a little malt house and some slaves. Until his participation in the Massachusetts Land Bank, which was outlawed by Parliament in the interest of preserving sound currency, Deacon Adams was prosperous, but, as a result of the bank's closing, he lost heavily and became embittered against England and the royal officials in the province. He achieved prominence in Massachusetts Bay politics and pressed hard for colonial rights through the "Caucus Club," which Sam was later to use to advantage. Samuel Adams's mother was a woman of severe religious principles; she instilled in her son the orthodoxy of the old Puritanism.

Sam attended the Boston Latin School; his schoolbooks with their annotations "by a thoughtful lad indicate the early bent and bias of his mind," which were later developed at college. He entered Harvard[4] at the age of fourteen and took an M.A. in 1743, having presented his thesis, based on the thinking of John Locke, in Latin:

4. Deacon Adams paid most of his son's college bills with flour and malt.

"Whether it be lawful to resist the Supreme Magistrate if the Commonwealth cannot otherwise be preserved?,"[5] reasoning with clarity in favor of the legality of an illegal action. He was destined for the ministry, in accordance with the wishes of his pious father and mother, but—though pious himself—felt irresistibly drawn to the world of politics.

At Harvard he studied the classics, rhetoric and natural philosophy. The college demanded that its scholars lead "sober, righteous and godly lives," and the drinking of brandy or rum in college rooms was strictly prohibited. During his senior year Sam was caught drinking; he escaped with a five-shilling fine although several of his companions were rusticated and degraded.

While Adams was at Harvard a religious revival, the Great Awakening, swept the country and the college became "a new Creature" filled with devout students who had experienced the "New Birth." In Boston the Great Awakening brought about "A Week of Sabbaths." Taverns and dancing schools were deserted for prayer meetings. Young men and women cast off their finery and walked along the fashionable Boston Mall wearing the somber dress seen during the heyday of Puritanism.

This religious revival was short-lived. The Congregational clergy soon found that, instead of bringing back the days of Cotton and Winthrop, the Great Awakening ushered in a wild religious frenzy. It proved to be the first of the backwoods revivals that were to sweep America during the eighteenth and nineteenth centuries. However, it left a deep impression on Samuel Adams. He cited the decline of Rome as a "dreadful example" of what might be expected in New England if the people lost the Puritan virtues, and compared the best days of the Roman Republic with the early period of New England settlement. Adams became known as the "Cato" of the American Revolution because he preached, year after year, the return to an

5. *The Pennsylvania Magazine of History and Biography.* Vol. I, The Historical Society of Pennsylvania, Philadelphia, 1877.

earlier and simpler way of life. Although he eventually achieved a large political following, few became enthusiastic about Adams's idea of turning back to Puritanism.

Following graduation from Harvard Sam was apprenticed to a man named Cushing, a merchant and politician who was head of the Popular Party. But Sam's interest was politics rather than business; he did so badly in the countinghouse that his employer returned him, regretfully, to his father, who gave him a thousand pounds and told him to make his own way. So Sam returned to the malt house, a well-established business. Deacon Adams died within a year, leaving his son a spacious old house in Purchase Street. Sam promptly ran through the thousand pounds.

Young Adams did not give promise of a great career; his scholastic standing wasn't really distinguished and he certainly showed no aptitude in business. Although he became a good mixer in political circles, he shied away from intimate friendships. Essentially a loner, Sam, in his twenties, was suspicious of people, of privilege and of wealth.

II

Adams Lights
the Fire

SAMUEL ADAMS'S POLITICAL INFLUENCE grew slowly, from small beginnings. He first won political office in 1746 when he was twenty-four and only recently graduated from Harvard; he was elected clerk of one of the Boston markets. Sam then fell upon a lean time, holding no office for some years. "Then, as now, it was customary to speak of 'poor Adams' as a failure. This verdict was shrewdly encouraged by Adams himself, who took every protection coloring his career."[1] In 1756 he was elected one of the collectors of taxes for the town of Boston, and his laxness led to one of the worst scandals attached to a signer of the Declaration of Independence. His easygoing attitude was popular with the taxpayers, to whom he

1. From *The Reluctant Rebels* by Lynn Montross. New York: Harper & Brothers, 1950.

listened sympathetically when they pleaded for delay, but he failed to collect what was due the town. In consequence, the tax collectors stood as defaulters to the town of Boston for £9,878. In spite of this scandal the citizens of the town liked Sam so much that they enthusiastically re-elected him.

For nearly a decade thereafter Adams made little political progress because in this period the French and Indians were burning up the New England frontier so that ambitious patriots like Sam, whose political success was to depend upon picking a quarrel with Parliament, found no support. When the French and Indians threatened the colonies, their loyalties were with England, their protector.

This was a bad time for Adams. In 1757 his wife, Elizabeth Checkley, died. By her he had two children who survived—Samuel, who became a surgeon in the Continental Army, and Hannah. Adams's children received a good education; Sam superintended their instruction with great care. No record exists of Elizabeth's life with her husband—only this epitaph which Sam wrote in the family Bible: "To her husband she was a sincere friend as she was a faithful wife. Her exact economy in all her relative capacities, her kindred on his side as well as her own admire. She ran her Christian race with remarkable steadiness, and finished in triumph! She had two small children. God grant they may inherit her graces!"

Adams was left with the two children and no income beyond his salary as a tax collector; he was indifferent about the making of money.

Sam Adams's fortunes improved when he attracted attention by vigorously defending his dwindling estate against seizure by the Land Bank Commissioners, who had harassed Sam's father. The Land Bank, a financial institution which served principally the agricultural community, and whose operations were based on paper currency, had grown to vast proportions, to the dismay of the merchants and lenders of money, who favored hard currency. When Parliament, responding to the pleas of the merchants and of Governor Jonathan Belcher, outlawed the Land Bank and declared its directors criminals, Deacon Adams had become involved in serious financial difficulties.

It was in the 1740's that, as a result of a severe depression in Massachusetts, money had become scarce, which led to the resurrection of the Land Bank paper-currency plan. The bank quickly became the rallying point of a political party bent on bringing government within the grasp of the common people. In the Massachusetts House of Representatives the Land Bank supporters achieved a large majority, and the royal governor became the only restraint upon people's fury against the merchants.

Deacon Adams, a director of the Land Bank who had invested most of his fortune in it, approved the attitude of the House. This body treated the Crown with "all possible rudeness and ill Manners" by ignoring royal instructions regarding paper money. "Few Crown officers doubted that, unless Parliament came to the rescue, royal authority would crumble and the colony would soon be 'ripe for a smarter sort of government' in which republicans such as Deacon Adams would hold the reins."[2]

The Land Bank controversy brought about a sharp break between the propertied class and the working people; the bank's rolls showed that artisans and yeomen predominated. In leading the Land Bank Party Deacon Adams foreshadowed his son's career.

By 1741 this party had reached the "height of its malignity" and rumors flew that thousands would march on Boston, insist upon cash for the Land Bank bills and demand grain from the merchants. What might have become the Great Massachusetts Rebellion was nipped in the bud by Governor Belcher when he rounded up the leading conspirators. The British Parliament responded to his pleas and those of the merchants by outlawing the Land Bank. All the directors were made personally responsible for the face value of Land Bank notes.

2. From *Sam Adams: Pioneer in Propaganda* by John C. Miller. Boston: Little, Brown & Co., 1936.

The Land Bank controversy dragged on and on, and in 1758, well after Deacon Adams's death and fifteen years after Sam had left Harvard, the Commissioners put his estate up for auction for the fourth time. When the General Court (the colony's governing body) ordered the estates belonging to Land Bank directors sold, Sam was furious; he attended the sale and threatened both the sheriff and the would-be purchasers. His dramatic appearance achieved its purpose; he then proceeded to attack the Commissioners for hounding him unjustly for debt, accusing them of bleeding the public with their inflated salaries. His onslaught by voice and pen was so successful that the Commissioners were forced to capitulate.

Sam Adams was destined to carry on the tradition set by his father, whose political anti-British views had been sharpened by the Land Bank affair. Its collapse had a deep effect on young Sam, accentuating his political radicalism; and at this time he entered into correspondence with John Wilkes, the famous British agitator. For Sam the spectacle of Wilkes becoming Lord Mayor of London and a member of Parliament was decidedly encouraging; Wilkes was a master at using both the mob and the press for his own purposes. He taught Sam a great deal in both these respects.

Adams's effective self-defense improved his ability in debate; his later success as a Revolutionary leader and as the mainspring of the revolt against England sprang from his fervor as a New England patriot. From that time on he was behind the inexorable progress of events that led up to the Battle of Lexington in 1775.

Nevertheless, he made little political headway until 1765, when the Revolutionary movement gathered steam because of the domination of Massachusetts by the "Shirlean faction." James Otis, a leader of the colonial cause in the legislature, called this a "motley mixture of High Churchmen, and dissenters who monopolized public office at the expense of the 'Country Party.'" Governor William Shirley had entrenched himself behind the "Court Party," made up of wealthy merchants, country squires and political appointees. The growth of Shirley's influence made Adams fear that the governor intended to destroy the colony's Charter rights.

Thomas Hutchinson, a fine example of the pre-Revolutionary American aristocracy and a man of learning and talent, was the "Prime Minister" of the Shirlean faction and later fought hard against Sam Adams and American independence. Hutchinson, handsome and elegant, set female hearts fluttering, and was determined to keep his class in power. He had an excellent mind and was not surpassed in his knowledge of the history of the province. Moreover, he was attached to America, the country in which he had been born and bred. Hutchinson, nevertheless, usually supported British colonial policy, and his attitude enraged the colonial radicals so that he was forced to barricade his home against the Boston mob. It is unfortunate that Sam Adams and Hutchinson both lived in Boston and that they were bound to have many dealings with each other. In the narrow streets of the town they were likely, any time, to come face to face; propinquity gave a nasty edge to their mutual dislike.

When Francis Bernard became royal governor in 1760 and Hutchinson was appointed chief justice, Massachusetts was enjoying a period of relative quiet and the colony appeared to be one of the least rebellious of His Majesty's American provinces. In fact, unlike many of the other colonies, Massachusetts had maintained a large army and made very substantial expenditures to help crush the French in the Seven Years' War. During this war the threat of Indian attacks from Canada held the Northern colonies close to the mother country; with its ending this bond was snapped. Moreover, they began to feel their importance, and agitation started against Bernard and Hutchinson. In Canada the spit-and-polish British soldiers had been resented by the colonists and the contempt of the redcoats for the Americans was not forgotten in Massachusetts Bay.

Through the Boston *Gazette* the Boston patriots "spit their Venom" against the governor. In the Caucus Club, which met in a garret, where the members drank flip and chose town officers, Sam Adams was prominent. He and his associates were considered by Hutchinson the "rabble" of Boston. Perhaps so, but Sam felt at home among the shipyard workers, masons and politicians who crowded into the attic.

Sam handled these encounters cleverly; he drank abstemiously at the Caucus Club and in waterfront taverns. In the evenings he'd meet with intellectuals to whom he quoted Milton and the classics. Of Sam, John Adams observed in this connection, "He was more cool, genteel and agreeable than common; concealed and restrained in his passions. . . . He affects to despise riches and not to dread poverty; but no man is more ambitious of entertaining his friends handsomely."

In eighteenth-century Massachusetts a large tavern acquaintance was essential for a politician; it was in the taverns that "bastards, and legislatores are frequently begotten."[3] Adams was fond of a pot of ale, a good fire and the company of laboring people of radical political opinions. With the soul of a Jacobin he found them, with their "tippling, nasty, vicious crew," good recruiting grounds for the mobs he later manipulated. Little by little Sam came to be regarded as spokesman for the common people of Boston; at the same time his social position gave him influence among middle-class citizens.

But despite the growth of his popularity among the rank-and-file Adams was not able at this time to gain much support for his cause against the British. After an unpromising start Hutchinson had become a popular chief justice and James Otis, a leading patriot of eccentric genius who was described as "a flame of fire,"[4] lost control of the House of Representatives as well as of the Massachusetts Council. "Even when the British unleashed another 'menacing monster' [in the form of the Sugar Act], Otis was unable to awake patriotic fervor in the province, outside of Boston."[5] Indeed, there was so little resistance that George Grenville, Chancellor of the

3. From *John Adams: A Biography in His Own Words,* edited by James Bishop Peabody. New York: Harper & Row, 1973.

4. Massachusetts Archives.

5. From *Sam Adams: Pioneer in Propaganda, op. cit.*

Exchequer, believed that Americans would swallow anything. He had not taken Adams into account, for the Sugar Act proved him one of the best watchdogs of colonial liberty. Sam protested vehemently, but ran into the opposition of the colonies' farmers, who were suspicious of the townspeople. It required the Stamp Act of 1765 to unite town and country and to make it possible for Adams to create formidable opposition in Massachusetts with Boston as its head. When that Act was enacted, William Pitt thundered: "I rejoice that America has resisted. . . . It is asked in Parliament, 'When were the colonies emancipated?' But I desire to know when they were made slaves."

Nevertheless, the Stamp Act was understandable—because England had, in the French and Indian Wars, incurred enormous debts and needed revenue from America, which had become wealthy in this period. It was not a hasty measure and was carefully framed to raise revenue from the colonies by taxing legal and commercial documents without damaging their economy. The Act had been read by the various colonial agents in London, who were given time to consult with their opposite numbers in America. None of them had much against it; yet, when passed, the Stamp Act raised an outcry of rage. Consequently, Grenville and the British Ministry were surprised by the reaction of the colonies and by the growth of colonial unity, which had seemed unlikely because of the great differences among them in manners, religion and interests.

Within a year of the passage of the Stamp Act the colonies were covered with societies determined to nullify it. They called themselves "Sons of Liberty" and they prevented execution of the Act by forming alliances from colony to colony, taking over much of the real power of government. Those Sons of Liberty who in Boston met in Hanover Square were known as the "Loyall Nine," and when Adams was entertained by them, he enjoyed a "very genteel Supper." Although neither he nor John Adams was a member of this group, Sam's connection with them was close; with their help he sparked the mobs which terrorized Boston. The Loyall Nine kept

The BOSTONIANS in DISTRESS.

Plate II.

London Printed for R. Sayer, & J. Bennett, Map & Printsellers, N.°53 Fleet Street. as the Act directs. 19 Nov.°1774.

their identity secret and let it be believed that the mob actions were spontaneous outbreaks.

But it was Virginia which sounded the alarm after the passage of the Stamp Act; at the instigation of Patrick Henry the House of Burgesses adopted the "Virginia Resolves" in 1765. They went so much further than the position taken by the New Englanders that Otis was, at first, shocked and pronounced them treasonable, although Adams, in the previous year, had anticipated the Resolves' doctrine of no taxation without representation. Oxenbridge Thacher, Boston representative on the General Court, exclaimed of the Virginians: "Oh yes, they are men! They are noble spirits! It kills me to think of the lethargy that prevails here." Thus the race between Virginia and Massachusetts for leadership against British tyranny came into being. This rivalry was important in precipitating the Revolutionary War.

The enactment of the Stamp Act came at a time when a severe depression had hit the colonies. So it was not difficult for Adams to raise an effective protest against such taxation by Parliament. Sam achieved political power when the wave of economic unrest swept over Massachusetts in that year of 1765. He was elected to the Massachusetts House of Representatives, or Assembly. However, his political prospects would have been very uncertain had not the British government stepped in and given him a much-needed lift by their decision at this juncture to raise new revenue from America.

Within two weeks of taking his seat in the House of Representatives Samuel Adams was elected to all the important committees and was recognized as James Otis's chief lieutenant. His pliableness and adaptability made him popular. With the "Massachusetts Resolves" of 1765, of which he was the author, he established his pre-eminence. Unlike other colonial state papers of this period, the Resolves omitted acknowledgment of Parliamentary sovereignty.

Although Virginia had led the way in protest against the Stamp Act, Massachusetts was first in riots. In the summer of 1765 Sam decided to terrorize Andrew Oliver, Hutchinson's brother-in-law, who had been appointed stamp master of Massachusetts Bay province. In August the Loyall Nine, probably obeying Adams's order, hung an effigy of Oliver on the Liberty Tree. Although the Crown officers at first considered this a mere boyish prank, they thought differently when the sheriff reported he could not remove the effigy without risk to his life. When a spectator asked Adams whom the effigy represented, he blandly replied that he did not know. "He could not tell, he wanted to enquire."

That evening a large mob paraded around the Town House, where the governor and Council were sitting, destroyed a building recently erected by Oliver—designed to be a stamp headquarters—and marched to Oliver's house, where they beheaded the effigy. In addition, the mob shattered Oliver's windowpanes and broke into his house in search of the stamp master, swearing to kill him when he was found.

The next day Oliver promised to resign his office.

The riot, which occurred on the fourteenth of August, was celebrated in New England every year as "the happy Day, on which Liberty arose from a long slumber." The Boston rioting encouraged similar demonstrations in other colonies and provoked violent resistance to the Stamp Act. These riots were serious but were tame in comparison with the eighteenth-century mobs of Europe—nothing remotely like the Gordon Riots in London took place in the colonies.

The rumor was spread by Sam and Otis that Hutchinson was the archconspirator of all because he'd planned the Stamp Act and sent it to England. Actually, Hutchinson had no part in the Act until it was passed by the House of Commons; it then became his duty, as chief justice of Massachusetts Bay, to enforce this law. When the Stamp Act was first proposed, Hutchinson had urged that it be given up.

Oliver's promise to resign satisfied Adams, but the "lower part of the mob" was "unwilling to lose their Frolick." Late that August the dreaded whistle was blown and the horn sounded, calling the mob out of taverns. Fortified by rum, they wrecked several buildings

New Hampshire

Stamp Master in Effigy
Massachusetts

(Wood engraving, 1829; from *Interesting Events in the History of the U.S.* by J. W. Barber)

belonging to customs house officers; then, warming to their work, made their way to Hutchinson's house. He wrote, "The hellish crew fell upon my house with the rage of devils." Had he not left the place, he probably wouldn't have escaped alive. It was a wild night; the mob gutted Hutchinson's house, robbed his strongbox and scattered the manuscript of his *History of the Province of Massachusetts Bay.* As the house caught fire, the citizens stood by, crying, "Let it burn!" Samuel Adams was probably not in that crowd, but had he been, he would have applauded. The colonists called on officials appointed to distribute the stamps to resign or be tarred and feathered; Hutchinson's worst enemies—James Otis and Samuel Adams—had not intended that the mob should go so far. Its violence boomeranged, and Hutchinson, for a time, became a martyr, admired especially in the rural districts.

On the morning after the riots Adams attended the town meeting and voted assistance to the magistrates in keeping order in the city. He was well aware of the political danger of an undisciplined mob and set about keeping it under leash—a particularly difficult task because the toughs of South Boston were constantly roughing up those of North Boston. Sam achieved the apparently impossible in bringing the two factions together at an enormous banquet, called the "Union Feast." To this Governor Bernard's reaction was that Sam had united the mob for his own political purpose. He was right; there was reason to distrust Adams for his clever dramatics before an impressionable audience. At all events the demonstration of "lovely Unity" marked the end of the mob as an unrestrained instrument in the Revolutionary movement.

Having forced the stamp master out of office and bottled up the governor in Castle William, the province's fort, Adams proposed to treat the Stamp Act as a "mere nullity." The customs house officers were forced to open the port without stamped clearances and the Act was ignored. Nevertheless, its brief existence had great effect in the colonies; a congress of representatives from the various provinces met in New York in November 1765 in order to protest to King and Parliament. Although not all of the colonies were represented, this meeting brought together men from many parts of the country and established the basis for the later Continental Congress. Even more significant: when, late in 1765, rumors started that the Stamp Act would be enforced by redcoats, the Sons of Liberty prepared to resist. On Christmas Day New York and Connecticut ratified a plan of mutual military aid against the British. Colonel John Durkee of the Connecticut militia asserted that he could bring ten thousand well-armed men to fight the enemy. The Whigs of Boston boasted that within a few days forty thousand New Englanders would be on the march to the city. In a letter to the Earl of Hillsborough, written some years later—in 1769—Adams wrote: "I think it necessary to suggest to your lordship that a militia of eight hundred thousand men, naturally brave and hardy, habituated from childhood to the exercise of arms, and animated with the enthusiasm of liberty or driven to despair, might refit a greater force than it will ever be consistent with the safety of this kingdom to send on an expedition so distant."

Opposed to this declaration was Thomas Cushing, another Bostonian, who warned Sam that the Southern colonies would not approve the raising of a large force. Adams disagreed vehemently, asserting that Massachusetts "would have the support and assistance of all the colonies." In angry response Cushing shouted: "That's a lie, Mr. Adams. I know it and you know that I know it."

Although Samuel Adams hankered for a fight, he and the Sons of Liberty did not then regard themselves as disrupters of the British Empire but rather as defenders of its Constitution. The Sons of Liberty believed the Stamp Act to be an encroachment by the House of Commons upon George III's "Crown and Dignity."

While the Sons of Liberty were toasting the King as they were threatening to annihilate royal troops, the British government repealed the Stamp Act. In John Adams's opinion this concession worked wonders with the colonists. He wrote: "The people are as quiet and submissive to government as any people under the sun; as

THE SONS OF LIBERTY PERSECUTING A TORY EXCISEMAN
(From mezzotint by Philip Dawe, 1774)

little inclined to tumults and riots, seditions, as they were ever known to be since the first foundation of the government. The repeal of the Stamp Act has composed every wave of popular disorder into a smooth and peaceful calm."

George III, years later, lamented Parliament's "fatal compliance" in repealing the Act.[6] Looking back, many British statesmen thought that Britain should have forced a showdown with the colonials in 1766, rather than given them nearly a decade to strengthen their defenses. But it is more likely that an attempt to enforce the Stamp Act would have been fatal to the Empire, for Americans were more united in '66 than in '75 and England had not, by then, fully recovered from the Seven Years' War.

"The repeal [of the Stamp Act] was greeted by riotous rejoicings in London, more hearty even than those in the colonies."[7] The Act had made Samuel Adams an important figure, so the Tories carefully examined this man who threatened them. What they saw was a middle-aged fellow, already stricken with palsy, wearing clothes rusty from the years. His friends saw him as a "plain, simple, decent citizen, of middle stature, dress and manners,"[8] who lived frugally and took pride in his poverty. Actually, Samuel Adams was an extraordinary, ordinary man,[9] extremely effective in a political meeting but not a stump orator. He never rested.

During the struggle between the House of Representatives and the governor Adams set aside days of fasting and so gave the Revolution the caste of a crusade. Peter Oliver, the brother of Andrew, the stamp officer, complained that Adams had perverted the clergy, who made their pulpits "Foam with Politics, Unceasingly sounding the

6. In fairness to the King the statement of John Clarke in *The Life and Times of George III* should be noted: "If the only alternative to repeal was to collect the tax by force, then George genuinely preferred to see the duties abolished."

7. From *The Outline of History* by H. G. Wells. New York: Macmillan Co., 1920.

8. From *John Adams: A Biography in His Own Words, op. cit.*

9. The phrase "an extraordinary, ordinary man" is from Donald Barr Chidsey's *The Loyalists.* New York: Crown, 1973.

Yell of Rebellion in the Ears of an ignorant and deluded People."
Sam had never forgotten the stirring days of the Great Awakening,
and his strongest wish was to bring back to New England seven-
teenth-century Puritan manners and morals. He regarded himself as
a restorer of the past rather than as an innovator; but he found it
harder to make New Englanders "Old Puritans" than rebels.

III

Adams and
Other Leaders
Press the Fight

IN THE EARLY PERIOD of unrest in Massachusetts James Otis was a more important figure than Samuel Adams. A hearty man, given to oaths, who treated religion lightly, his "mobbish eloquence" made him an enemy of the British. Not until Otis was hit on the head in 1769 by a British Commissioner in a tavern brawl, causing brain injury and bringing on incipient madness, did he lose a dominant position among the New England Patriots. While Sam was un-equaled as a propagandist, Otis was an original political thinker. Otis, a radical, but nevertheless a stout imperialist, would have been shocked to learn that his *Rights of the British Colonies Asserted* was considered a textbook of rebellion. Indeed, it was according to the concept of natural law, as set forth in this book, that the Revolution was defended by Otis and Adams.

Otis believed that the ills of the British Empire could be cured if the colonists were represented in Parliament. Adams, on the other hand, declared that representation of America was "utterly impractical." With his realistic mind he saw that accepting the idea of federation would make effective argument for colonial independence of the Crown impossible. He took the position that only when the colonial assemblies were recognized as having the sole taxing power in the colonies would they and the mother country "long flourish in one undivided Empire."

Otis was a strange, confused person; his radicalism conflicted with his conservative background. Otis, said John Adams, resembled Martin Luther in that he was "rough, hasty, and loved good cheer," while Sam Adams, like Calvin, was "cool, abstemious, polished, and refined, though more inflexible, uniform, and consistent." In the opinion of Peter Oliver, Otis was "rash, unguarded, foulmouthed, and openly spiteful," while Sam Adams resembled no one so much as the Devil.

James Otis's enemies sneered at him when he entered politics in 1760 and called him insane; even his friends admitted that his conduct was eccentric. John Adams considered Otis "fiery and feverous"; he was, in fact, either very gay or very despondent. Otis's affection for the British Empire tormented him, but when he returned from the Stamp Act Congress, he spoke so violently against Hutchinson as to put the latter in danger. Yet only a few days later Otis outraged the Whigs by maintaining that the way to keep peace in the colonies was to take away the Massachusetts Charter, fill the Council with royal appointees, and quarter British troops in Boston. In the House of Representatives he was sometimes a wild-eyed radical; sometimes a dyed-in-the-wool conservative. The life of this violent, talented man ended (in 1783) appropriately; he was struck by a bolt of lightning. One of his chief contributions to the Revolutionary movement was his declaration, "Taxation without representation is tyranny." It epitomized the aims of the Patriots, who resented that the colonies—so important a part of the British Empire —should not be represented in Parliament. Many Englishmen who were indignant about the "rotten borough" system in England felt the same way; they bitterly resented that the cities of Manchester and Birmingham were taxed although they were not represented in Parliament, while Old Sarum, an uninhabited heap of stones, sent a member to the House of Commons. Undoubtedly the American Revolution gave impetus to subsequent electoral reform in Britain.

Among the early colonial leaders none was more significant than Benjamin Franklin, whose visions of the future challenge those of H. G. Wells or Jules Verne. As early as in 1754 Franklin drew up a plan that called for a Grand Council to meet annually in Philadelphia to regulate Indian trade and to have sole power of legislation on all matters affecting the colonies as a whole. To these ends it would levy taxes, enlist soldiers, build forts and nominate all civil officers. Its laws were to be submitted to the King for approval; the royal veto, to be effective, would have to be exercised within three years. Known as the Albany Plan, this proposed confederation afforded a valuable precedent for the expanded and more suitable Federal Constitution of 1788.

Another example of the boldness of Franklin's conceptions was his anticipation of the speedy peopling of the Mississippi Valley, for at this time few colonists had crossed the Alleghenies. And he thought the time not far distant when America would predominate in the British Dominions and when the seat of Empire might be transferred to this country, and England would become subordinate.

Franklin even foresaw the use of airborne troops! In 1784 he wrote: "Where is the Prince who can afford so to cover his country with troops for its defenses, as that 10,000 men descending from the clouds might not, in many places, do an infinite deal of mischief before a force could be brought together to repel them?"

John Hancock was another important Patriot leader in this period; when Adams brought him to the Patriot Club in 1765, Hancock was a young man of fashion with one of the largest fortunes in the country. Sam guessed that his hankering for popularity and susceptibility to flattery could be turned to advantage. Not only could Hancock give prestige to the Patriot cause; he also might help Sam in his financial embarrassments as tax collector. Both of these suppositions proved to be right; Hancock became the financial godfather of the Whigs. Moreover, his important business activities gave employment to a thousand workers whose votes could be counted on since they would not offend their employer by casting ballots against Sam Adams. The Tories accused Adams of "serpentine Cunning."

Sam made a coup when he attracted Hancock to his cause; a man of such substance was just what the Patriots needed. But, in time, Hancock's allegiance wavered, and had he not been up against financial difficulties when the British applied pressure to colonial trade, he might have gone over to the Tories.

The Whigs made impressive gains at this time and James Otis was elected speaker of the House of Representatives; Adams, the clerk. In this position Sam exerted great influence; having access to all the papers reporting debates to the House, which had hitherto been privileged, he promptly used them for propaganda and made them public by printing them in the newspapers.

Adams held a grudge against the Council, whose members were elected by the House of Representatives,[1] for the part they had played during the Stamp Act struggle. The Council had remained loyal to the governor, and Otis shrieked that the Upper House had become "an infernal Divan." Following the upset of the Tories the Council was divested of many of Governor Bernard's staunchest supporters; it had not undergone a purge of such proportions since 1741, when the aristocrats were turned out by Deacon Adams and the Land Bank Party.

Samuel Adams's quarrel with Great Britain was no revolutionary act but was based on his interpretation of constitutional law. He held

1. The legislature of Massachusetts (known as the General Court) consisted of a House of Representatives (or Assembly)—the Lower House—and a Governor's Council—the Upper House. These bodies corresponded to the House of Commons and the House of Lords in England.

that the British Parliament was violating the Massachusetts Bay Charter, granted in 1691, when it levied internal taxes on the province, since it lacked authority to do so, the Charter being specific in what it allowed the colony. Adams considered the Charter as the contract the philosopher John Locke (whose works were the sourcebook for the American Revolution) had prescribed between the sovereign and his people.[2] Unfortunately, it is doubtful whether George Grenville, or any of the First Lords who dealt with the colonies, knew or cared what was in the Charter of Massachusetts Bay.

Adams's political acumen made him powerful; in opposing British encroachments his strategy was to use every conventional and legal avenue of redress and only when they had failed to resort to extralegal measures. Sam was the "Man of the Town Meetings," and his membership in the Massachusetts Assembly, starting in 1765, did not prevent his attendance at town meetings, where general as well as local problems were discussed.

By 1768 Adams had reached the conclusion that there was no hope of redress from the British government and that Parliament had no right to legislate for the colonies on any subject. But he was too good a politician to admit this publicly; the time had not yet come.

Since an English army was on the way to enforce colonial submission, Sam believed in the necessity of expressing many of his views to the colonies and of inviting European alliances. However, he shrewdly realized that he could not press for armed resistance in Massachusetts, since no other colonial leader who later took part in the Continental Congress thought as he did in 1768—nor for many years thereafter. In fact, Jefferson said in 1775, three months after the battle at Lexington: "We have not raised armies with designs of separating from Great Britain and establishing independent states.

2. The colonists assented only to British taxation for the purposes of regulating trade and navigation.

Necessity has not yet driven us into that desperate measure."

Adams distrusted the fine world. Although he was well educated, his plainness was in contrast to Otis, Warren, Cushing and Hancock. At town meetings he was at his best, and it was largely due to his influence that the town meeting, originally designed to pass on strictly local matters, took on all the important functions of government in the province. Besides, everyone who wished to attended the meetings and no attention was paid to their qualification as voters. "The spirit of anarchy," Hutchinson, newly installed as governor, observed in 1770, "is more than I am able to cope with." He excoriated the mob and its instigators, like James Otis "with his mob-high eloquence" and, even more, Samuel Adams, who had supplanted him; Hutchinson thought Sam abler, and considered that there was not "a greater incendiary in the King's dominion, or a man of greater malignity of heart [or one] who less scruples any measure however criminal to accomplish his purposes."

Between town meetings Sam would pour himself out in the newspapers; he would harangue the laboring people, sitting with a ship's carpenter or a shopkeeper. He sharply distinguished the mob from the workingmen but, nevertheless, used it as a political instrument; the mob's ardor could be turned on and off to suit the politics of its directors.

The burning of the ship *Gaspée* in Narragansett Bay took place in 1772. The ship's captain had been overzealous in executing the British-imposed revenue laws. When the *Gaspée* went aground, a Patriot party from Providence attacked and burned her.

The handling of this episode showed evidence of Adams's prestige—also of his genius for taking full advantage of every opportunity for propaganda. When he was asked by the prominent men of Rhode Island what to do in this crisis with the Crown, Sam replied by saying that the Rhode Island Assembly should send a circular letter to the other colonies protesting the *Gaspée* incident and the punitive measures being discussed by the King's Commissioners.

TOWN MEETING.

(Engraving from *M'Fingal*, by John Trumbull, 1795)

It is interesting, in view of Sam Adams's violent dislike of George III's government, that in June 1773 he drafted a very respectfully worded petition to the King expressing the hope that "your Majesty will be so graciously pleased to remove them [Thomas Hutchinson and others] from their posts in this Government and place such good and faithful men in Their stead as your Majesty in your great Wisdom shall think fit." Although Adams was terribly in earnest, he never displayed an excess of zeal or rage, as did Warren and Josiah Quincy, Jr.

In the summer of 1773, in a series of essays in the Boston *Gazette,* Sam urged the project of a Continental Congress as the only salvation of the colonies. At this time the cause of the Whigs was in trouble; many were getting tired of the controversy with England.

In September, two months before the occurrence of the Boston Tea Party, Adams wrote in the *Gazette:* "I beg leave to offer a proposal to my countrymen, namely, that a Congress of American States be assembled as soon as possible; to draw up a Bill of Rights, and publish it to the world; choose an Ambassador to dwell at the British Court to act for the united Colonies. . . ." Three weeks later he raised the question of how the colonies should force their oppressors to proper terms. His answer: Form an independent state—*an American Commonwealth.*

This was certainly a radical proposal, and previously Sam might have been expected to press for representation in Parliament. Such a request could possibly have been granted since the idea of American representation was apparently not distasteful to Westminster. But Sam believed that the time required to cross the Atlantic—two months—would make it impossible for the colonists to instruct their delegates.

Adams was made chairman of the Assembly committee on the state of the province of Massachusetts. The committee was divided about taking effective measures against the British, and Sam, with half-closed eyes, purred for conciliation until the doubtful were completely deceived.

The Patriots now feared the arrest of Adams and of his prominent supporters, but the British hesitated, fearful of the consequences. Governor Hutchinson said: "The Lords of the Privy Council had their pens in their hands in order to sign the warrant to apprehend Adams, Molineux and other principal incendiaries, try them and, if found guilty, put them to death."[3]

When, in 1774, New York proposed a Continental Congress, it left Adams cold, although he had recently advocated this; he felt that quicker action was essential and feared that Tories and lukewarm Whigs in a congress would wield sufficient power to block effective progress. On the other hand, the country as a whole supported the idea of a congress, having noted that the Crown had sent a general, Thomas Gage, to replace Governor Hutchinson. Accordingly, the First Continental Congress was called into session at Carpenters' Hall in Philadelphia on September 5, 1774, with fifty-six delegates representing all the colonies except Georgia.

Samuel Adams was always behind the scenes; he was not chairman of the town's committee set up to drive out the British soldiers in 1770, he was not among the Mohawks at the Boston Tea Party in 1773, although he organized them, and at the last town meeting before Lexington it was Warren who was apparently the central figure, although directed by Sam. His influence was pervasive. In *The American Revolution* John Fiske writes: "The more we reflect upon the slowness with which the country came to the full consciousness of its power and importance, the more fully we bring ourselves to realize how unwilling America was to tear herself asunder from England and how the Declaration of Independence was only at last resorted to when it had become evident that no other course was compatible with our self-respect; the more thoroughly we realize all

3. "There is some reason to suppose that he [Adams] was subsequently offered, as a bribe to keep silent, a pension of 2000 guineas and a patent of nobility in the American peerage which was projected." From *Samuel Adams* by James K. Hosmer. Boston: Houghton, Mifflin Co., 1885.

this, the nearer we shall come toward duly estimating the fact that in 1768, seven years before the battle of Lexington, the master mind of Sam Adams had fully grasped the conception of a confederation of American states independent of British control."

As the session of Congress wore on, the resentment toward New England increased. While Richard Henry Lee and Patrick Henry of the South were ready for independence, there was no discussion of this during the early stages; Sam Adams, impatient, began to entertain the idea of declaring independence for the New England colonies, hoping the rest would follow in time.

Something had to be done and Sam had the answer—to shake off the yoke of British law. From here on Sam worked for this, preparing men's minds in secret. The methods he followed were not always open; he did not invariably admit his true sentiments but often protested, on behalf of the town or province, loyalty to the Crown. Radical though he was, Adams always focused his attack on Parliament rather than on the King. One of the reasons for Adams's success as an anti-British agitator was his diligence in training promising young political recruits—men like John Hancock, Josiah Quincy, Jr., and Joseph Warren.

Samuel Adams was a man of opposites; in religion a narrow Puritan but in manner genial; rigid in his opinions but in the expression of them often compliant; conservative yet radical. He could be a most agreeable host—and gentle, concealing his strong passions. Pretending to despise riches, he nevertheless wished to entertain his friends handsomely—a difficult aim since Sam had few visible means of support. He was, indeed, a complex character and many Boston patriots distrusted him while others admired him. Thomas Jefferson offered Sam a unique tribute: "I often asked myself, is this exactly in the spirit of the patriarchal Samuel Adams? Will he approve of it? I have felt a great deal for our country in the times we have seen, but individually for no one so much as yourself."

Adams's eloquence was limited, his second cousin, John, being far his superior; while basically sincere, he sometimes resorted to false dramatics. Yet John Adams said of Sam: ". . . upon great occasions, when his deeper feelings were excited, he erected himself, or rather nature seemed to erect him, without the smallest symptoms of affectation, into an upright dignity of figure and gesture, and gave a harmony to his voice which made a strong impression . . . the more lasting for the purity, correctness and nervous elegance of his style."

Nor was Sam at his best as a writer—though he wrote voluminously. He had a clear style based on the classics, but the intensity of his conviction sometimes made him narrow. It was as a tactful, and sometimes Machiavellian, manager of men that he starred; the world has seldom seen a man so able in his methods of swaying a meeting. His sense of timing—when to advocate controversial action—was extraordinary, and Adams, though emotional and passionate by nature, knew just when it was necessary to conciliate rather than press.

A loyalist printer painted a different picture of Sam Adams, calling him "The would-be Cromwell of America," and he wrote: "Mr. A's character can be defined in a few words— He is a hypocrite in religion, a republican in politics, of sufficient cunning to form a consummate knave, possessed of enough learning as is necessary to disguise the truth with sophistry, and so complete a moralist that it is one of his favorite maxims 'The end will justify the means.' "

A notable feature of Sam Adams, in common with the other Founding Fathers, was his respect for the law and property. His services to colonial America were outstanding, and the phrase "Father of his Country," invariably attached to George Washington, can also be applied to Adams, the innovator who united the colonies and drove them to rebel.

The Adams household, in 1764, had consisted of Sam's two children by his first wife, a black slave girl and a Newfoundland dog which could not bear the sight of the British soldiers, the "lobsterbacks." In that year, when Sam's political prospects were uncertain, he remarried. Elizabeth Wells brought him no dowry but was a wonderful manager of his needy household, a steadfast supporter of her husband's political activities, and, generally, the ideal helpmate. She made his stipend as clerk of the Assembly serve for food and, through the generosity of friends and her own ingenuity, provided indispensable clothes for the family. It was said of her that she had waited twenty-eight years for a husband and "was determined to keep this one well contented." They lived frugally. "He [Sam] says he never looked forward in his life," recorded John Adams with Yankee incredulousness at his cousin's carelessness, "never planned, laid a scheme, or formed a design of laying up anything for himself or others after him."

The Sam Adamses were known for their religious strictness; prayers were said before breakfast, passages read in the evening and the Sabbath rigidly kept. Though not a Puritan in the sense understood by Winthrop and Cotton, Sam was considered in pre-Revolutionary Boston "the last of the Puritans." He turned his religion to political advantage, organizing singing societies among Boston mechanics, where he displayed, as one member observed, "an exquisite ear for music and a charming voice."

IV

Life in the
American Colonies
in Adams's Time

THE COLONIAL WORLD Samuel Adams was born into was a divided one—divided not only in its attitude toward England but also as between North and South, for conditions of life were very different in these two parts of the country and travel from one city to another was incredibly time-consuming. In New England nonconformist Puritan tradition was still an influence, while in Virginia near Anglicans predominated. New England was largely populated by small farmers—yeomen; in contrast, the South was a land of large plantations. The yeomen were aggressively assertive (any man was as good as another), unlike the tradition of Virginia and its neighboring colonies, where the landed, slaveowning class, so close to the eighteenth-century Whig aristocracy of England, was established.

America was a land of opportunity: Henry Shrimpton, a London brazier, so expanded his interests and activities after settling in Boston in 1639 that he left an estate of £10,000 twenty-seven years later. By 1776 the colonial aristocracy had endured for more than 150 years in the oldest regions. It created no resentment; the aristocracy consisted of men who, through shrewdness and ability, had stayed at the top. After all, the colonists chose a Virginia aristocrat, George Washington, as commander-in-chief.

At the time of the French alliance in the Revolution six thousand Frenchmen came to this country to fight alongside the colonists. Many of them were keen observers and their comments on our way of life—some of them made during the period immediately after the war—give a good picture of colonial attitudes and prejudices.

The visitors found America harsh, with an uneven climate and violent storms. They reported very bad roads and, everywhere, unsightly tree stumps two feet high—symbols of the forest conquered. They saw stumps left to rot and front yards with no flowers, but planted with wheat and corn.

They did find grandeur in the American scenery. The country they traversed would be unrecognizable to us today; porpoises played in the East and North rivers around New York. Baltimore, with only a few thousand inhabitants, was ill-paved, with scarcely a dozen lamps in the whole town. .

French travelers were amazed at the high scale of living. Wages for laborers—such as those Sam Adams consorted with—and servants were much higher than in Europe. But they agreed that, as one journeyed south, the people looked less well off. In fact, they were shocked by the living conditions of slaves and of the wan, ragged whites. In contrast, Southern gentlemen's houses were spacious and elegantly furnished—but with few books on the shelves.

Moreau de Saint Méry, a French nobleman, found that the longer he stayed in America, the less the inhabitants appeared to resemble Europeans. He was constantly surprised at the equality of people of different rank; he would see a member of Congress seated next to a laborer in the same coach. These things were extraordinary to a Frenchman. In the colonies equality was not just a matter of conversation as in the salons of Paris or among the philosophers; it was a way of living.

Another Frenchman, François de Barbé-Marbois, wrote: "We went through pretty little villages without ever having an official come up, hat in hand, and with a mawkish expression beg us, in the name of the thirteen states, to get out of our carriages and let him inspect them." There were in the colonies no seignorial rights for those entering or leaving districts; this applied not only to Samuel Adams's New England domain but to the whole country.

Barbé-Marbois and his companion, when walking through the New England countryside, encountered a farmer and questioned him: "Who possessed the high and low justice in the district? How much rent did he pay to the lord of the village?—Was he allowed to hunt or fish?—Was the tithe heavy and forced labor frequent and painful?

"There is an element of fantasy in the scene. At all these questions —the man started to laugh—He told us that justice was neither high nor low in America but perfectly fair and equal for everyone, and we could not make him understand what sort of beings lords of the village were."[1]

Barbé-Marbois didn't see a single pauper nor meet a "peasant" who was not well dressed. Foreigners were upset that they could find no difference between maid and mistress. "Luxury," wrote one, "has penetrated to the cottage of the workingman." These travelers could not have observed the slaves, of which there were half a million in the colonies; nor the numerous white, indentured servants. Another was surprised that everyone could read and write and noted that newspapers and gazettes were numerous and kept people well informed.[2]

1. From *The Miracle at Philadelphia* by Catherine Drinker Bowen. Boston: Little, Brown & Co., 1966.
2. This observation was made along the Atlantic seaboard; in the backland there were no schools.

Foreign visitors were intrigued by the colonial women. Moreau, strolling along Philadelphia streets, observed: "One can see four hundred young persons, each of whom would certainly be followed on any Paris promenade. These maidens, so charming and adorable at fifteen, unfortunately will be faded at 23, old at 25, decrepit at 40 or 45." (Presumably from excessive childbearing and hard manual work.) He was amazed that women left their hair a natural color— rouge was proscribed, as was powder; in fact, the prudery of most American females struck him as unconscionable. Marbois wrote that, upon a gentleman inquiring if French ladies rode horseback and hearing that they did, "like men—all the women blushed, hid themselves behind their fans and finally burst into laughter." Certain words were taboo in the presence of ladies: garter, leg, knee, skirt. American women divided the body into two: from the head to the waist was stomach, the rest was ankles. "In God's name how could a doctor guess the location of a female ailment? He is forbidden the slightest touch," writes Moreau. "His patient, at the risk of her life, leaves him in the vaguest doubt."

Another Frenchman, the Marquis de Chastellux, considered that there was an awful solemnity about young American ladies and noted that when one of them, at a soirée, was urged to sing, she sat on a chair, straight as a poker, her eyes fixed on the floor. "One waited until her voice began to proclaim that she was not petrified."[3]

The French visitors found in America a provincial society where there had not been time to acquire the poise and badinage of Parisian salons. They found what they were bound to find in a young country—rigidity. Easy laughter, gaiety and the absence of prudery belonged to an older civilization. In Boston a lady who had invited Sam Adams to dinner described him as incapable of carrying on a conventional conversation, observing that he appeared "too uneasy to sit quietly in his chair."

3. These comments must have been made about Northern women, for in the South the ladies were flirtatious and vivacious.

A few years after the Revolution Thomas Cooper, a well-known scientist and theologian, observed: "I do not think America a place for a man of pleasure." Even in Philadelphia, Cooper knew of only one professed gentleman, i.e., an idle, unoccupied person of fortune. "The time is not yet come," he observed.

In Massachusetts and other New England states, where there existed a strong movement for general education, the authorities had resorted to legal coercion to attain this goal. In consequence these colonies had achieved the nearest approach to the present American system of free education then known in the English-speaking world. The American mind in 1775 was well stocked. Not only did the colonists read almanacs and newspapers; a substantial number, like Adams and his Harvard friends, also knew the major writings of ancient and modern times. The Duc de La Rochefoucauld wrote of them: "All these people busy themselves with politics, and from the landlord to the housemaid they all read two newspapers a day."

Southern colonies did the least to provide educational opportunities, and in both North and South girls were neglected. By general consent the simplest elements of learning sufficed for their predestined role of wives and mothers.

It was observed that Americans were creating a new language; New Englanders said *dew* for "do," *tew* for "two." Thomas Jefferson was sensitive to this and reacted against English reviewers who criticized the adulteration of the language by American words. "The new circumstances in which we are placed," Jefferson wrote to Washington, "call for new words, new phrases."

At the time of the Revolution the colonies boasted nine colleges, where learning tended toward the utilitarian. The practical application of experimental theory and utility "was part of the âme républicaine, Ben Franklin its prophet and Philadelphia its natural center." In New York and Philadelphia professional training in medicine was provided, which developed some bold, imaginative doctors. Nevertheless, they prescribed curious remedies like red bark and opium;

they bled their patients for fevers. Women in labor were bled because they were thought to have too much blood. And health conditions in the towns were shocking; filth was thrown into the streets, wells were contaminated by backyard privies. Typhoid, malaria and smallpox infested the cities, especially in summer.

There was so much to be done that there was little time for leisure and for cultivation of the arts. Literature was not a means of livelihood as in Europe—rather an amusement. Franklin admitted that the New World was no place for artists and observed that the gifted ones in America, like Benjamin West, John Singleton Copley, Gilbert Stuart and Charles Peale, went to Europe, where they could be properly rewarded.

The settlers, mostly coming from the uneducated classes in the Old World, were not consciously inclined to aesthetic appreciation. But unconsciously they showed a simplicity of taste that delights the modern eye. They made for their houses objects that were attractive as well as functional, their folk art reflected the simple lines and proportions of the craftsmanship of the Middle Ages. Gentlefolk demanded elegant furniture, mostly of English design. Native artisans—Paul Revere, Duncan Phyfe, William Stiegel of Pennsylvania —turned out fine work: silver, furniture and glass. Beauty was most deliberately pursued in gardens; amid the harshness of untamed nature, people sought solace and serenity in the fragrance of gardens.

Architectural styles mirrored the new taste in England after the London fire of 1666. Colonial architects avidly read manuals derived from Christopher Wren and, for a time, followed the British; but quite soon American builders developed Colonial Georgian, which flourished by the second quarter of the eighteenth century. This came about because the available building materials were different from those in England, as well as the climate; timber for stone in New England, in New York brick. Southern planters liked pillared front porches to protect themselves from the heat.

Colonial art, though derived from the British, had a special glow because it reflected the fresh perspective of a new country.

Americans tried in many ways to reproduce English civilization, and the tendency gained strength as rivalries between the colonies hindered development of a common American loyalty. Often the relationship with London was stronger than with colonial neighbors; there were boundary disputes and no uniform currency. To Andrew Burnside, an English visitor a few years before the Revolution, "Fire and water are not more heterogeneous than the different colonies in North America. Nothing can exceed the jealousy and emulation which they possess in regard to each other. We thought that civil war would rage from one end of the continent to the other should the colonies break with Great Britain."

New England, like Sam Adams, was deeply moral. Although the sixteen churches in Boston no longer dominated the city's life at the time of the Revolution, they were still a powerful force; most of the ministers were dedicated liberty men, "the black regiment," as they were called. Adams said: "There is seldom an Instance of a Man guilty of betraying his Country who has not before lost the feeling of moral Obligation in his private Connections." Yet Puritan New England allowed bundling or tarrying. This custom, imported from the Old World, permitted a suitor and his sweetheart to woo in bed, provided (in theory) that they did not take their clothes off or have sexual relations, and provided the parents consented. It was a convenient custom, especially in poorly heated houses.

For amusement outside the home, Americans—except in Boston —went to the theater; the early performances were given in taverns and warehouses, but in due course theaters were built in most of the principal cities. The colonists, in developing a new society, never lost sight of the saving element of fun. Indeed, the action of the Continental Congress in binding its members by "sacred ties" to discourage "all Horse Racing, and all Kinds of Gaming, Cock Fighting, Exhibition of Shews, Plays and other expensive Diversions and Entertainments" was evidence of the wish for recreation in colonial times.

> "If I were asked to what the singular prosperity and growing strength of the American people ought mainly to be attributed, I should reply—to the superiority of women."
>
> —DE TOCQUEVILLE

Colonial women were brave. At the height of King William's War in 1689 a band of Canadian Indians swooped down on Haverhill, Massachusetts. Mrs. Hanna Duston, who was taken prisoner along with several other women and children of the settlement when the redskins retreated north, escaped; but not before she was obliged to tomahawk a dozen or more of her captors. She returned home with a handful of their scalps and explained: "You might not have believed me if I hadn't brought home the proof."

Christine Zellers, wife of a German immigrant who had settled near Lebanon, Pennsylvania, in 1745, planned and superintended the construction of a fort or "house of refuge" for her fellow colonists in the region. Shortly after it was completed a band of Indians attacked, swarming through the windows one morning when her husband and the other male settlers had left to work in the fields. Instead of panicking, she lifted the ax with which she was chopping up logs for kindling and beheaded the first three redskins to appear. Terrified, the others fled. Christine then dropped the bloody weapon and proceeded to sweep the hearth, which was apparently next on her list of daily chores. When the men returned from the fields and congratulated her on her heroic deed, she merely remarked that any American woman faced with the same problem would have reacted in the same way.

Colonial women were conspicuously industrious. Whether the patriotic female Patriot chose to make soap or gunpowder or both, whether she replaced her husband in the fields or in the schoolhouse, whether she chose to second him on the battlefield or to spy for him, she worked incessantly for the cause.

In such a society the qualities of thrift and industry were developed rather than the graces of a cultivated civilization.

V

The British
Tighten the Screw

THE CUSTOMS COMMISSIONERS set up under the Townshend Acts
of 1767 were to be assigned to a headquarters in Boston, and when
Samuel Adams heard this, he and the Sons of Liberty planned to fall
upon them and march them to the Liberty Tree, where they could
choose between resignation or facing the mob. However, lacking
support from the other colonies, this plan had to be abandoned and
the Commissioners, upon arrival, were merely accompanied by a
mob carrying placards with "Devils, Popes and Pretenders" in-
scribed on them. The mob did them no harm; it was a "trained
mob," obedient to Adams.

The Commissioners, who were gay blades, found Boston insuffer-
ably dull. They managed to amuse themselves by organizing parties,
balls and concerts, scandalizing Adams and giving the town its first
taste of night life. At first these parties were unpopular, but soon

Bostonians found them so enjoyable that Sam was forced to endure the sight of Whigs as well as Tories drinking and dancing with the Commissioners.

Adams and Otis set about to oppose the Commissioners by proposing to the House of Representatives that a Circular Letter be sent to the other colonies, acquainting them with the measures taken by Massachusetts against the Townshend duties. To their dismay, the House rejected the Circular Letter plan, thereby greatly pleasing Governor Bernard. Not long after, however, when the country delegates had gone home, Adams and Otis reopened the matter and succeeded in persuading those remaining that the Circular Letter be sent out. It denounced the Townshend Acts as violating the principle of no taxation without representation, attacked any move by the Crown to make colonial governors and judges independent of the people and proposed united colonial action. Bernard declared the Letter seditious and dissolved the General Court. However, the Letter conceded the "superintending power" of Parliament, a position which John Adams could not understand. He felt that the Circular Letter should have stated that Parliament had no authority of any kind in America. He was right in principle, but in 1768 the time was not yet ripe for throwing off Parliamentary authority. It is interesting that Sam, the agitator, understood this and that John Adams, the future Federalist President of the United States, apparently did not. Sam, nevertheless, was by then privately convinced that independence was the only solution to the struggle with the mother country.

The effort by the British government to compel the colonies to renounce the Massachusetts Circular Letter aroused a fever of opposition. Sam believed that no step taken in his colony had more united the country.

The rioting which broke out in Boston in 1768 against the Commissioner of Customs and the subsequent arrival of British troops thoroughly aroused Adams. "The caution and reserve which Adams usually displayed in transforming American discontent into revolutionary fervor were characteristics acquired through many years of self-discipline. By nature, Adams was passionate, excitable and violent, but he rarely allowed these qualities to appear in public."[1] The crisis of 1768 caused him to shed his "serpentine Cunning" and make a rash appeal to arms, reviving the plan to fight off the Crown's troops before they could gain a foothold. War enthusiasm flared up and remained hot until it was learned that British troops were within a few days' sail. Then it subsided—suddenly. The country areas were inclined to cool the Boston hotheads. The *New Hampshire Gazette* declared: "We are not to act like Rebels. Scorn the thought. We have a good King and his royal ear is not wilfully shut against us."

In default of the legislature, dissolved by Governor Bernard, Sam Adams called the Massachusetts Convention, which met in Faneuil Hall in September 1768; it was the counterpart of the House of Representatives. The rural moderates gave the Convention a conservative caste; even the city Patriots showed restraint due to the refusal of the New York Sons of Liberty, as well as the country delegates, to join in the fight against the Crown. Adams sensed the pulse of the colonies and drafted a cautious letter to the colony agent that was wholly acceptable to the Convention. He brought himself to write that George III should regard the Convention as "a fresh token of the loyalty of our respective towns to his Majesty, their attachment to his government, and love of peace and good order."

On October 1, 1768, the redcoats landed in Boston under the guns of men-of-war and marched unopposed to Faneuil Hall, making the Boston Sons of Liberty a laughingstock throughout the colonies. As for the British politicians, they became convinced that New England's threats could be disregarded. But the effect on Adams was profound; after the landing of the British troops, he felt that armed resistance was the necessary course of action.

The troops found an outwardly peaceful town, but beneath the surface it was in ferment. According to John Adams, "The life of a redcoat wouldn't have been safe in any street or corner of Boston.

1. *Sam Adams: Pioneer in Propaganda, op. cit.*

Nor would the lives of inhabitants be much more safe. The whole militia was on watch and guards were everywhere. No man was exempted and J. A. served watch at the State House, with his musket and bayonet."

The British demanded quarters for their soldiers, but the selectmen and Council called their attention to the law forbidding such a requisition until the barracks at Castle William were filled. The troops, therefore, had to camp on the Common. This was the beginning of discomforts for the redcoats, who were scorned in a town where three-quarters of the inhabitants were against them. The little boys would jeer at the "lobsterbacks."

Samuel Adams demanded the removal of British troops from Boston town to the Castle. It was at Faneuil Hall that Sam addressed Lieutenant Governor Hutchinson, who, having consulted a Colonel Dalrymple, stated that one regiment should be ordered down to the Castle. Again, John Adams describes the scene: "With a self-recollection, a self-possession, a self-command, a presence of mind that was admired by every person present, S. A. arose with an air of dignity and majesty, of which he was sometimes capable, stretched forth his arm, though even quivering with palsy, and with an harmonious voice and decisive tone, said, 'If the Lt. Gov. or Col. Dalrymple, or both together, have authority to remove one regiment, they have authority to remove two, and nothing short of the total evacuation of the town by all regular troops will satisfy the public mind or preserve the peace of the province.'

"These few words thrilled through the views of every man in the audience, and produced the great result. After a little awkward hesitation, it was agreed that the town should be evacuated, and both regiments sent to the Castle. These troops were called with humor and sarcasm 'Sam Adams' regiments."

Adams regarded his speech at Faneuil Hall, addressed to Lieutenant Governor Hutchinson, as his finest.

Yet, despite Sam's triumph over Hutchinson, this was a low period for the Boston Patriots; the Nonimportation Agreements between the colonies had broken down when the British Ministry promised a partial repeal of the Townshend duties. Since the repeal of the Stamp Act Adams's dream of a united America had never seemed so remote as when the colonies fell to quarreling with one another over the blame for the breakdown of the Nonimportation Agreements. In fact, the collapse of these Agreements was a bad reverse for the Massachusetts Whigs; for the first time Tories could drink toasts to Samuel Adams's downfall with prospect of success.

An era of good feeling with the British started, and for nearly two years the American colonies were not even mentioned in House of Commons debates. For Adams the worst blow came when, in 1770, the British government made the blunder of installing Thomas Hutchinson as governor in place of Bernard. Adams, though he had detested Bernard as a tyrant, infinitely preferred him to Hutchinson, "who worked in the dark with gloves."

Tories realized that, unless Adams's hold on the General Court were broken, Massachusetts Bay would not be "as decent and polite" as other colonies. Sam's position was solid until he demanded that Hutchinson return the General Court from Cambridge, where it had been moved by orders of the Crown, to Boston. Murmurs against Adams's leadership were then heard among the Whigs; worse, James Otis led the mutiny against him. Otis had been carried out of Boston in a strait jacket in 1770, but within a few months reappeared, temporarily cured of his madness, and was re-elected to the House of Representatives, where he reaffirmed his reverence for the Crown.

Otis's revolt was upsetting to Sam but less a threat to his leadership than John Hancock's rapprochement with the Tories. The latter's financial support of the Whigs—and of Sam Adams—had been expensive so that he was now inclined to pay less attention to politics and more to his business, which was not doing well. He concluded that a man of his position should not be associating with penniless politicians who were willing to ruin every merchant in Boston to gain their ends. In 1771, when Hutchinson learned that Hancock and other "heroes of liberty" were ready to turn their backs on Adams, Hancock was ready to switch his allegiances. But, as a pupil of Sam, he'd learned the unwisdom of burning his bridges and so made alliances with both parties, sitting on the fence until the winning side could be determined. Although Hancock did not quite desert, his attitude badly worried the Whigs. This devious politician did not actually break with Sam and, while making up to Hutchinson, continued to give him occasional lifts in his chariot, leaving the door open to future reconciliation.

Another blow for the Patriots, and particularly for Sam Adams, occurred when John Adams decided to quit politics and retired to his legal affairs and farming in Braintree. Likewise, the patriotic spirit sank in other colonies and most people lost heart; as the Tory Party kept gaining, the Whig rank-and-file pressed for a reconciliation between Adams and Hancock, with the result that the two were brought together. As proof of the accord Hancock commissioned John Copley to paint his and Sam's portraits, which Hancock hung side by side in his drawing room.

The new relationship was not to endure indefinitely for the two men were not real friends. Hancock was always eager to snatch the leadership from Sam, whom he regarded as a plebeian wire-puller; Adams distrusted Hancock as a flighty young man of fashion who was decidedly un-Puritan.

When, in 1770, Lord North and the Tory Party came into power, Adams knew that coming to terms with the mother country was impossible (not that the British Whigs, as a party, had been of much help to him). Furthermore, Sam had a low regard for the man Massachusetts had decided to make its London representative— Benjamin Franklin. He distrusted Franklin as a Tory at heart, and his cousin John considered him a scandalous old rake. Worse, the Ministry made Hutchinson, Sam's pet hate, financially independent of the colonial legislature by paying his salary as governor out of the revenue collected by the Commissioners of Customs. This interference with the rights of Massachusetts Bay was resented throughout the colonies and the spirit of revolt was reawakened.

The sides had been taken. Opposing the Patriots were the King's supporters in England, and in the colonies the Tories, the "best families," who, as a rule, took the King's side either from selfish motives or from conviction. Britain prepared for the next step and Boston was marked as the most rebellious of American cities.

VI

The Boston Massacre,
the Tea Party and
the Consequences

ONLY HALF A DOZEN PEOPLE lost their lives during the whole period during which British regiments were quartered in Boston; a tribute to the discipline of the soldiers and to the moderation of the citizens. Yet all the time there was a deep undercurrent of distrust —and sometimes hatred—between the people and the soldiery. Boston citizens were annoyed by drunken brawls and by the scores of prostitutes who had followed the regiments across the ocean.

The British soldiers were a rough crew, underpaid, disciplined by the fear of cruel punishment. Generally forced into service by press gangs who found them drunk in English pubs, or serving in the army to avoid serving jail sentences, they were treated by their officers like animals. To compensate for the low pay British troops were permitted to loot, but in America this was forbidden because the officers feared offending American Tories. Looting took place, however, despite brutal punishments ranging from violent floggings to death. Other incidents infuriated the Patriots, from hacking John Hancock's fence to taking liberties with pretty Yankee women. Even more irritating was the moonlighting by the English soldiers, who took on odd jobs at very low pay.

The occupying soldiers suffered most from boredom; there was nothing to do except the daily drill. As the months passed, the troops were ripe for any affray, while the lower-class inhabitants became increasingly angered by the soldiers' noisy ribaldry. From these conditions developed the Boston Massacre.

On March 2, 1770, insults were exchanged between a ropemaker, Nicholas Ferrier, and a "lobsterback." The soldier left the scene only to return shortly with men from his regiment, headed by a tall Negro drummer with a cutlass. Ferrier received a cut on the head; then, supported by nine or ten of his associates, he reported, "We beat them off, with wouldring sticks."

For three days the two regiments in town remained angry; another affray started when a soldier and a barber's boy quarreled. A crowd gathered near the State House, snowballs and sticks were thrown; the maddened soldiers retaliated by shoving their bayonets toward the crowd.[1] Then came the command, "Fire." It is not known who gave that command; Captain Preston, commander of the British detachment, did not. The incident resulted in the death of five inhabitants and produced angry repercussions throughout the colonies which unified them for a time to a degree not previously attained. A spark had been thrown into tinder.

In retrospect, it seems remarkable that two of Boston's leading radicals, John Adams and Josiah Quincy, should have defended Captain Preston and six of his men when they were arrested for murder. The court let five go free and punished two by having their hands branded. Sam Adams was outraged and "retried" the case in the

---

1. The British troops were permitted to fire, even if fired upon, only at the command of the Civil Court of Boston.

Boston *Gazette,* signing his articles "Vindex The Avenger." He was determined to win a propaganda victory and, in his passion to convince the world that the soldiers had wantonly attacked the mob, disregarded the evidence.

First reports of the Boston Massacre reaching England caused a commotion in Parliament. Some members stated that the soldiers had violated civil authority by firing into the mob. Motions of censure were introduced; they were defeated, but to what extent this reflected opinion in Parliament is a question in view of the corruption of English politics at this time.

Things quieted down after the Boston Massacre; the radical Patriots lost control of the Massachusetts House. One man, Sam Adams, did not let up; he said at the time: "Where there is a spark of patriotic fire we will enkindle it."

Between August 1770 and December 1772, he wrote more than forty articles for the Boston *Gazette.* Night after night, a lamp burned late in the study off his bedroom. Friends, passing in the small hours, could look up at the yellow square of window light and comfort themselves that Sam Adams was busily at work against the Tories. . . . His style in this period was at times severely reasoned, more often impassioned; the content was unfailingly polemical, partisan and, on occasion, willfully inaccurate. As the conflict with Britain deepened, his accusations increased in violence.

It was in October of 1772 that Adams wrote: "Let it [the subject of colonial rights] be the topic of conversation in every social club. Let every town assemble. Let Associations and Combinations be everywhere set up to consult and recover our just Rights."

So started the organization of the Committee of Correspondence. The year before, Sam had written to a political colleague with the suggestion of such a committee: "a sudden thought which drops undigested from my pen." He went on to say that a Committee of Correspondence should promote union not only among the colonies but also with men of similar views in England.

Adams had set himself a Herculean task, for he found the Patriots mostly indifferent—Thomas Cushing, Hancock and Samuel Phillips, as well as the most influential among the selectmen. But he discovered allies in other towns, like young Elbridge Gerry in Marblehead. He set out to persuade the town meeting in Boston to appoint a Committee of Correspondence. The town records of Boston state:

> It was then moved by Mr. Samuel Adams that a Committee of Correspondence be appointed, to consist of 21 persons, to state the rights of the colonists and of this Province . . . and to communicate and publish the same to the several towns and to the world as the sense of the town. . . .

The motion was long debated and finally carried late at night. However, Adams's close colleagues did not support him and refused to serve on the committee; they regarded the plan as both useless and trifling. Nevertheless, the Boston Committee of Correspondence included, as time passed, well-to-do merchants and professional men.

The first meeting of the Boston Committee of Correspondence took place on November 3, 1772, with twenty-one members and James Otis in the chair. According to the motion by which the committee was constituted there were three things to be done: (1) the preparation of a statement of the rights of the colonists; (2) a declaration of the infringements and violations of those rights; and (3) the sending of a letter addressed to the towns in the province and to the world giving "the sense of the town." The document, when printed and distributed, had great effect, and the towns appointed similar committees to respond to Boston's Committee of Correspondence. According to James K. Hosmer, author of a nineteenth-century biography of Samuel Adams, "The documents ought to inspire the deepest reverence. They constitute the highest mark the town meeting has ever touched."

The recommendations of the Boston Committee of Correspondence (BCC) were printed and read at town meetings. The first pamphlet was called "The Votes and Proceedings of the Town of

Boston"; it was placed in the hands of opinion leaders and public officials all over the province. Simplicity was the virtue of the BCC's writings, and Sam Adams must be given credit for this.

Adams's plan for the Committee of Correspondence showed vision. When it was started, no one, not even his friends, foresaw its consequences; within two years similar committees were carrying on intercolonial correspondence as far south as Charleston. Governor Hutchinson called it "such a foolish scheme that the faction must necessarily make themselves ridiculous." On the other hand, one of the ablest Tories, Daniel Leonard, wrote about Sam, presumably in connection with his Correspondence project: "This is the foulest, subtlest and most venomous serpent ever issued from the egg of sedition." The Boston Committee of Correspondence was also stigmatized in the press as "a set of atheists or Deists, men of profligate manners and profane tongues."

Actually, the Virginia Patriots had anticipated Adams; as early as 1768 Richard Henry Lee had suggested that the colonies establish committees for intercolonial correspondence, but it was Sam's success with the plan that convinced Lee, Patrick Henry and Thomas Jefferson to put it in operation. Almost every colonial assembly followed.[2] Without the work of the committees it is doubtful whether the First Continental Congress could have been held in 1774.

Indeed, the BCC grew to be so effective that Hutchinson became alarmed; revolutionary opinions were spreading very fast. He kept waiting for Parliament to squelch the revolting colonists, and finally could wait no longer. Thereupon he called the Assembly; he wanted this body to "avow or disavow" the town proceedings, which he described as "tending to mutiny and rebellion." In this aim he

2. The recommendations from the various town committees varied significantly. In 1773 a circular letter was sent by a "committee" of slaves. "It may have been drawn in conjunction with Samuel Adams and John Pickering (of Salem) who were forwarding efforts toward ending slavery." From *Revolutionary Politics in Massachusetts* by Richard D. Brown. Cambridge, Mass.: Harvard University Press, 1970.

completely failed; the Assembly took no action.

While there is no question that Samuel Adams was a radical, his conception of the relationship between the colonies and the mother country foreshadowed that of Britain and the Dominions today. His slogan for Massachusetts was "Freedom from every legislature on Earth but that of the province," and he believed that the mother country and provinces would "live happily in that connection, and mutually support and protect each other."

Adams's Committees of Correspondence, in spite of the ridicule they had inspired in their early stages, had spread throughout the colonies. The next step was for them to assemble, and it only remained for the British to create an issue; they promptly obliged, although Lord North, the Prime Minister, tried to persuade the King to use restraint. Up to a point he succeeded; in the Rhode Island case the matter of the *Gaspée* was dropped, but George could not be restrained from showing that he was King by reviving the taxation issue, upon which all the colonies were bound to unite. He insisted upon the principle of the tea tax although it brought less than £300 a year to the British exchequer.

None of the colonies would accept the taxed tea, although they depended upon tea as Americans depend on coffee today. They made their own "Liberty Tea," a poor substitute made of sage, currant or plantain leaves. To try to deal with this situation the British made their tea cheaper than the Dutch despite the duty of 3 pence per pound; they reasoned that the Americans would buy the lower-priced tea and would thus be tricked into admitting the principle of the duty. Their reasoning was wrong, and the colonists objected to the East India Company's monopoly as well as to the displacement of the old tea merchants by the company's consignees.

In the fall of 1773 several British ships, loaded with tea, sailed for the four principal colonial ports—Boston, New York, Philadelphia and Charleston. Upon getting news of this the whole country was ablaze. In New York and Charleston the consignees of the tea were asked to resign—and did so—but in Boston they refused. The eyes

WOMEN PROTEST TEA TAX

of all the colonists turned to Boston as the battleground where the great issue would be settled. Encouragement came from all over the country; in Philadelphia the church bells rang and there was rejoicing in the streets. A letter from the men of Philadelphia to those of Boston had this to say: "Our only fear is lest you may shrink. May God give you virtue enough to save the liberties of your country."

On November 28 the first of the tea ships sailed into Boston Harbor. The Committee of Correspondence promptly met and Sam Adams invited the committees of neighboring towns to hold a mass meeting at the Old South Meeting House, where it was unanimously voted that the tea be sent back to England—an illegal resolution since the ships had already entered the customs limits. It was further resolved that the citizens of Boston and other towns would see that these resolutions were put into effect "at the risk of their lives and property." Sam had copies of the resolution sent to the other colonies and to England. Thereupon a mob disguised as Mohawk Indians[3] and Negroes rushed to the waterfront and emptied 342 large chests of tea into the harbor.

The Boston Tea Party achieved the calculated effect of infuriating the British government. It made Lord North apoplectic so that when American liberty was mentioned, he would "vomit forth" horrid threats against the rascally colonists. The King, also, was aroused and English public opinion was behind him. It was this violent reaction that made the comic-opera affair of the Tea Party important.

In Massachusetts there was great exultation. Sam Adams exclaimed, "This is the most magnificent movement of all. There is a dignity, a majesty, a sublimity in this last effort of the patriots that I greatly admire." In contrast, some historians have described the

3. However, Ebenezer Stevens, a general in the colonial artillery, denies this accepted version. He wrote: "I was among the persons who destroyed the Tea in Boston Harbour—None of the party were painted as Indians." But he adds: "Some of them stopped at a paint-shop on the way and daubed their faces with paint." From *Erasmus Stevens and His Descendants* by Eugene R. Stevens. New York: Press of Tobias A. Wright, 1914.

Boston Tea Party as "the tea riot of Boston," a highly inappropriate phrase since the Tea Party, organized by Sam, was orderly and passions were curbed by sound reason. The colonists had reached a point where they had to preserve their free way of life.

"Had the tea been landed," writes a late-nineteenth-century historian, William Gordon, "the union of the colonies in opposing the Ministerial scheme would have dissolved."

When news of the Tea Party reached England, Lord Germain, who was to become Secretary of State for the Colonies, reacted: "This is what comes of their wretched town meetings—these are the proceedings of a tumultuous and riotous rabble, who ought, if they had the least prudence, to follow their mercantile employment and not trouble themselves with politics and government, which they do not understand." "These remarks," observed Lord North, "are worthy of a great mind."

North now proposed five drastic measures for curbing the Americans, and at this moment the Opposition spoke up. Edmund Burke, Charles Fox, Isaac Barré and others maintained that the tax on tea must be removed since otherwise insurrection would follow. But North persisted, saying, "To repeal the tea duty would stamp us with timidity."

North took these five measures:

> The Boston Port Bill, whereby no ships would be allowed to enter the port until the rebellious town paid indemnification for the loss of the tea[4]
>
> Annulment of the Charter of Massachusetts, which meant destruction of her government and concentration of all power in the British governor
>
> Provision that any magistrate, soldier or revenue officer indicted for murder would be tried in Great Britain (George pressed for this measure over North's objection)

4. This stupid and outrageous act not only deprived a substantial number of men of their livelihood but mortally wounded their pride .

Removal of legal obstacles to the quartering of British troops

Extension of the boundaries of Canada (by the Quebec Act) south
to Ohio, thus defying the territorial claims of Massachusetts, Connecticut, New York and Virginia; the region to be governed by a viceroy
with dictatorial powers

A month after these measures had been passed, in April 1774,
Governor Hutchinson was supplanted by General Gage, who was
authorized to close the port and so begin to starve the inhabitants
into good behavior. He was also authorized to use his discretion in
allowing his soldiers to fire on the citizens. These incredibly repres-
sive laws were contemplated by George III "with supreme satisfac-
tion."

Thereafter the sovereign authority of Great Britain was never-
more recognized by the citizens of Massachusetts. The various towns
in the colony had achieved unity, with the result that the Committees
of Correspondence, which had performed such a great service, were
supplanted by action on the part of local communities acting together.

Again opposition flared up in Parliament. The Duke of Richmond
spoke: "I wish from the bottom of my heart, that the colonists may
resist and get the better of the forces sent against them." But few
Englishmen believed that the Americans would resist, or that Massachusetts would be supported by the rest of the colonies. They were
wrong; conventions in most of the colonies declared that Boston was
"suffering in the common cause." Cattle, sheep, cartloads of wheat,
provisions of every kind were sent overland to the beleaguered city.

It is interesting that the otherwise forward-thinking Ben Franklin
should have written from London at this time, suggesting that, after
all, Boston had better pay indemnification for the destroyed tea. This
evoked the comment from American Patriots, "Don't pay for an
ounce of the damned tea!" As usual, strong support for New England came from George Washington, who declared: "If need be, I
will raise a thousand men, subsist them at my expense and march
myself at their head for the relief of Boston."

Nevertheless, more than expressions of sympathy were required to ensure the concerted action of all the colonies. The proposal for a Continental Congress was made by the Sons of Liberty in New York and was immediately taken up by the Virginia House of Burgesses, Massachusetts being invited to set the time and place for the meeting. These decisions were made at a convention of Committees of Correspondence from the towns of Massachusetts, organized by Samuel Adams, who locked the door of the meeting room and put the key in his pocket. He acted wisely for some of the more timid members attempted to leave the meeting. However, one of them pretended illness and was permitted to exit; he promptly called upon General Gage, who attempted—without success—to break up the meeting.

The proposals were overwhelmingly passed and the Assembly elected Samuel and John Adams, Thomas Cushing, Robert Treat Paine and James Bowdoin as delegates to the First Continental Congress.

Passing through New York City on the way to Philadelphia, Sam found little to raise his spirits; there was a strange "delinquency and backwardness" in the city, he thought. The Sons of Liberty seemed lukewarm, and it was doubtful whether the party in power in New York would support the Congress. Moreover, the attitude of Philip Livingston and other New York delegates was distinctly cool to the New Englanders. And the Southern Tories were muttering: "Boston aims at nothing less than the sovereignty of the whole continent"; Samuel Adams, who was distrusted as a leader of mobs, was the target. The Pennsylvanians were quoted by John Adams as saying: "You [the Massachusetts delegates] must not utter the word independence; if you do, we are undone, for independence is as unpopular in all the middle and south as The Stamp Act itself."

The fact that Sam was a strong Puritan also antagonized the High Church Episcopalian delegates from the South. He was well aware of this and, by supporting the motion that Dr. Duché, a prominent

Church of England clergyman, open the Congress with prayers, Sam made a clever move which pleased and surprised the Southerners.

After these men had set off for Philadelphia it was Dr. Joseph Warren who took the most active part in the direction of Patriot affairs in Boston; he was a strong supporter of Sam Adams and a close friend of his. A young man of bravery, courtesy and a brilliant mind, he was one of the most important and boldest Massachusetts Revolutionary leaders—a fine, incorruptible figure and a charming, civilized person. Hancock, also, was of great value to the cause on account of his wealth, although, in comparison with the others, he lacked intelligence and strength of character. Yet he was generous despite his vanity.

Warren drew up the "Suffolk County Resolves" (September 6, 1774), which set up a legislature independent of General Gage. The Resolves declared, among other things, that a king who violates the chartered rights of his people forfeits their allegiance and that collectors of taxes should refuse to pay Gage's treasurer. These Resolves were thereupon endorsed by the Congress, which pledged aid to Massachusetts should armed resistance become inevitable. Simultaneously, Congress urged that a policy of moderation be continued and that the British be left to fire the first shot. In opposition, Joseph Galloway, a conservative from Pennsylvania, proposed a written constitution for North America which would formally unite the colonies and the mother country. Galloway's Plan of Union, creating an American Parliament with power of veto over its British counterpart, came close to passing until it was opposed by Patrick Henry.

On the twenty-seventh the Massachusetts Provincial Congress chose a Committee of Safety with Warren as chairman and directed them to collect military stores. Soon thereafter a militia was organized and officers appointed. A special portion of the militia was set apart and called "minute-men," since they would be ready to assemble at a moment's notice; every village green in Massachusetts became a drill ground. The men were not unused to arms for a third of them had fought in the French and Indian Wars.

New Englanders now appeared to Sam Adams like the Puritans of old; they prayed as they cleaned their muskets.

VII

The Fight
Against George III:
A Civil War

THE POPULARLY ACCEPTED MYTH about the start of the American
Revolution is that in the early battles around Boston outnumbered
forces of colonial militia fought gallantly, firing with deadly effect
from behind trees and rocks, against a superior number of well-
trained British regulars; that America was unjustly taxed by a stupid
king; and that colonial leaders encouraged the people to fight for
independence.

These assumptions, mostly false, deserve critical examination:

At the Battle of Lexington on April 19, 1775, which took place
some twelve miles from Boston and initiated the fighting in the
Revolution, the Americans *were* outnumbered, but by the time the
British were retreating in near rout to Boston from neighboring
Concord on the same day, our militia reinforcements from the farms
around there made the colonial force larger than the enemy's. And,

as the Americans laid siege to Boston, they numbered twice the British. Furthermore, while many of the colonials fought gallantly, quite a few skulked in the rear. It should be noted, also, that at Lexington the Americans stood on the village green, a perfect target for the regulars; only later that day did they fire from behind rocks and trees—a tactic the British considered distinctly unsportsmanlike. The Americans' marksmanship was poor except for a detachment of New Hampshire sharpshooters at the Battle of Bunker Hill.

It is true that the colonists were unjustly taxed in the sense that they had no say about taxation. However, the assumption that George III was stupid is contradicted by his shrewdness in manipulating Parliament. His great faults were obstinacy and narrowmindedness.

Finally, contrary to the popular assumptions, although the colonial leaders did encourage the people to assert their rights, they were very far from agreed about striving for independence even after the fighting had started.

The population of the colonies in 1774 was 2,600,000, mostly agricultural. The cities were small, Philadelphia, the largest, boasting about 30,000 people. New York's population was around 20,000, Boston's 17,000, and that of Charleston, the leading center for music, theater and the other arts, 12,000.

America was a rich country—richer by far than any other British colony; the people lived well and the epicure Brillat-Savarin observed that he had dined no better anywhere than at the house of a Connecticut yeoman. Yet America depended on England for manufactured goods until the Non-Importation Act was passed by the colonies in 1774; industry then sprang up immediately, and within a year a single Massachusetts town made eighty thousand pairs of women's shoes. In New England the basic pre-Revolutionary industries were shipbuilding, agriculture and fisheries.

The historian George Otto Trevelyan writes: "So great was the value of America for fighting purposes. But, in peace and war alike, her contribution to the wealth, the power, the true renown of Eng-

land exceeded anything which hitherto had marked the mutual relations of a parent State and a colony." Trevelyan goes on to observe:
"A member of what in Europe was called the lower class had in
America fewer cares, often more money, than those who, in less
favored lands, would have passed for his betters."[1]

The political alignments were confusing. Richard B. Morris esti-
mates that at the start of the fighting the percentage of Patriots
probably ran 40 to 50, that of Tories (also called Loyalists or Royal-
ists) about 20 percent—the remainder being fence-sitters who, in the
words of John Adams, "didn't give a damn one way or the other."
As in the Civil War, families were split, father fighting against son
and brother against brother—Benjamin Franklin's son was a prominent Loyalist whereas his grandson, Temple, served as secretary to
the Patriots' Peace Commission at Paris in 1782. The wealthy merchants of New York were mostly Tory,[2] but the dividing line between the two factions in America was not always wealth; George
Washington, John Hancock, Philip Schuyler and Charles Carroll of
Carrollton were reported to be the four richest men in America at
the outbreak of the war.

To be a Patriot did not mean that one was a leveler or a radical
theorist. Generally sympathetic with the Whig Party in England, the
Patriots' aim was to obtain political rights for Englishmen abroad
rather than to recast the social system. The American Loyalist differed mainly from the Patriot in his loyalty to the Empire; he did not
consider himself a member of the British Tory Party.

New York contained more Loyalists than any other colony,[3] but
there was a substantial number of them in Boston. As the splendidly

1. From George Otto Trevelyan, *The American Revolution*. New York: McKay Co.,
1964.

2. American Tories were the most persistent enemies of liberty, more so than their
English counterparts.

3. Virginia had the lowest percentage of Loyalists—surprising because this was an
aristocratic community of large landowners who might be expected to support privilege. But these men were accustomed to order their lives without interference; the
spirit of liberty was strong in them and their views were shared by most of the colony's
inhabitants.

trained British troops began to arrive in Boston Harbor from England in 1768, the Loyalists never doubted victory. Their opinion was shared by the King's troops, one of whose regimental officers observed: "As to what you hear of their [the colonists'] taking arms, it is mere bullying and will not go farther than words. Wherever it comes to blows he that can run the fastest will think himself best off."

Many Americans regarded the Loyalists with a loathing that they never felt for the British regulars. At the beginning of the war, efforts were made to win over the Loyalists, but that attitude soon changed to whipping, tarring and feathering, confiscation of property and banishment. To an extent unrealized the war of liberation within the colonies was a civil conflict. Toward the end of the Revolution two thousand American Tories fought a like number of Patriots at the Battle of King's Mountain and the only Britisher who took part was the commander of the Tories.

When Howe was forced to evacuate Boston in the spring of 1776, the Patriots swarmed into the city, burning Tory homes. Hostile brothers hate with more venom than anyone else, and from Maine to South Carolina American Tories were lashed, pelted with rotten eggs and forced to get down on their knees to damn the King.

At the end of the Revolution there were eight thousand American Loyalists in uniform in the British Army, while the American forces under Washington then numbered barely nine thousand under arms, and desertions were increasing. Loyalists were, of course, considered traitors by the Patriots; their land was seized, many were exiled. After Yorktown, remaining Loyalists went to the wilds beyond the Alleghenies, to Canada and to England. Those who emigrated to Britain expected to be greeted as heroes, but nothing of the sort took place. To their consternation they discovered that considerable numbers of Englishmen had favored the Revolution, speaking for it and even raising money for the cause. Other Britishers offered sympathy at first, but then wondered whether these visitors were not quitters, after all. The exiles felt they could never return to America; but, in fact, a number of them did and those who

were well heeled and had good connections were received with considerable cordiality.

In contrast to the quality of the American statesmen, Lord North, the Prime Minister, fat and genial, was weak and subservient to the King, as were other Tory leaders. But on the Opposition, Whig benches of the House of Commons, Edmund Burke, Charles James Fox and William Pitt were liberal as well as brilliant; they all spoke eloquently in favor of the American cause. Trevelyan writes: "Pitt's private correspondence clearly indicates that the keenness of his emotion, and the warmth of his advocacy, were closely connected with a profound belief, that, if America were subjected, Britain would no longer be free."

The most vehement pleader of the American cause in Parliament was Colonel Barré ("damn-your-eyes Isaac Barré"), a fierce Irishman of French descent who had been with Wolfe at Quebec.

An acute observation on the nature of the American Revolution was made by the American historian, Frederick Jackson Turner, who hailed it "as the most effective presentation of the fact that the struggle for independence was, in truth, a phase of a struggle between two English parties, fought on both sides of the water; in the mother country in the forum, in the colonies on the field of battle."

The Revolution was also an international war; France joined the colonists and German mercenaries—Hessians—were hired to fight by the British. Of the French involvement Trevelyan takes a jaundiced view. He describes the transactions by which Beaumarchais furnished arms and other supplies to the colonies and tells of the negotiations leading to the Franco-American alliance; he finds this a story of French duplicity and fatuity. The French government, which thought to buy victory cheap, "was submerged in an ocean of bankruptcy where it was destined miserably to perish."

British prestige, also, fell. At the end of the Seven Years' War in 1763 England was the most powerful country in the world; moreover, she enjoyed a large measure of goodwill from her European neighbors. Everywhere she was respected, admired and imitated, but by the time the American rebellion had lasted a year Great Britain could count on no friend, no ally. No wonder, for in the British accounts of the war, except those by supporters of the colonial cause, there is no lofty purpose to be found; they simply stated the necessity of military victory over the rebels.

George III's leadership proved fatal. He was thirty-six when the Revolution started, tall, handsome in a way, but with thick lips and vapid blue eyes. In his childhood George's mother had repeatedly admonished him: "George, be a real king!" This injunction sank in. George became obsessed with the technique of manipulating Parliament and, having turned Pitt and the Whigs out of office, ran his ministers like the manager of a team. "George worked at being a king with dogged persistence."[4]

George, although obstinate, was industrious, sober (in an age when many English nobles drank their gallon of strong wine daily) and possessed a talent for administration. On the other hand, he had little imagination and was incapable of understanding any problem requiring generalizing capacity. Yet he could discern immediate ends and pursue them doggedly, and he was able to gain men's confidence by a show of interest. He would then turn them adrift when it suited him. He surrounded himself with sycophants and, in attaining his ends, used every means at his disposal.

George hated Pitt and his New Whigs, who were out to reform Parliament, which was almost totally unrepresentative of the country due to the "rotten borough" system. Had Pitt been successful, he would have deprived George of the means of corruption. The King's political attitude toward the New Whigs and Pitt explains his violent support of the policy of taxing the colonies, for if the American position that there should be no taxation without representation were granted, it would have become necessary to admit the principle

4. From *Those Damned Rebels: The American Revolution as Seen Through British Eyes* by Michael Pearson. New York: G. P. Putnam's Sons, 1972.

of Parliamentary reform at home. Indeed, George III can be considered the principal element in the struggle between the colonies and England. He was glad to force the issue of representation in America rather than in Britain because this enabled him to persuade most Englishmen that the Americans were rebels and so obscure the real issue.

When he ascended the throne in 1760, Parliament had assumed what it considered a controlling position with the King, but, soon, George became the dominant force. For the next twenty years he summoned and dismissed ministers almost at pleasure.

Within five years from the beginning of his reign George III showed symptoms of extreme eccentricity. "His correspondence reveals a monarch who, had he lived today, would be the perfect sitting duck for the amateur psychoanalyst. A manic-depressive, rigid, moralistic and censorious, he appeared to casual acquaintances to be equable and reserved, whereas his intimates knew him to be hot-tempered, tense and loquacious, to bear grudges, and to make a virtue of obstinacy."[5] He was not really mad, he only acted so; it is believed that he had a disease of the urine called porphyrinuria. When he broke down in 1788, using foul, indecent language, and was put away in a strait jacket and forcibly kept from the ladies of the court, he was suffering from this disease. In spite of his frightening handicaps, however, George III showed courage at times and, while he was almost malignant in his vendettas, *could* be a good loser once he had accepted defeat. To John Adams, the first postwar envoy to England from the United States, he said: "I will be very frank with you. I was the last to consent to the separation; but the separation having been made and having become inevitable, I have always said, and will say now, that I would be the first to meet the friendship of the United States as an independent power." Yet, shortly thereafter, when Adams

5. From *The American Revolution Reconsidered* by Richard B. Morris. New York: Harper & Row, 1967.

presented Jefferson, George turned his back on the two of them.[6]

The American victory put an end to the personal government of the King. Americans—in effect—fought the battle of freedom for the Old World as well as the New; the Revolution was only part of a world struggle in which England was involved. From Spain and Holland came threats of invasion; there was war in India; and at certain stages of the Revolution the British Ministry considered the American war secondary.

Clearly, the colonies had many supporters abroad. When the much-maligned Marie Antoinette had fallen on evil days, even one of her enemies said of her: "It was the Queen of France who made the cause of America a fashion at the French court"—not quite a fair statement since Louis XVI was a better friend of America.

As the Revolution gathered momentum, America's Founding Fathers clarified their purpose. At issue was not simply successful revolt against the King; it was necessary to devise a form of government completely opposite to the absolute rule of George III, in which "executive privilege" ran wild. It was also necessary to establish a system of checks and balances, of separation of powers.

The Founding Fathers did their work well. William Pitt declared that the papers prepared by the First Continental Congress were unsurpassed by any state papers ever composed in any age or country.

6. From *Thomas Jefferson* by Fawn M. Brodie. New York: W. W. Norton, 1974.

VIII

The Fighting
Starts

THE IRREVERSIBLE MOMENTUM initiated by Samuel Adams gained in intensity when Thomas Paine produced *Common Sense* and *The Crisis,* which awakened the public mind and prepared the people to call for independence. And it was on the twenty-third of March, 1775, that Patrick Henry made his famous speech in Richmond, saying: "The war is inevitable and let it come! The next gale from the north will bring to our ears the clash of resounding arms! I know not what course others may take, but as for me, give me liberty or give me death!"

Early in the morning of April 19, 1775, twenty-one companies of picked British soldiers marched out from Boston, across the rolling countryside of Middlesex, with the object of seizing some powder at Concord, twenty-one miles away by road, and arresting Samuel Adams and John Hancock.

The enemy contingent represented about one-sixth of General Gage's army garrisoning Boston. Gage was probably the most peaceful occupying general in history; his wife was a handsome American and, according to gossip, she dominated him.

Gage had begged Lord Hugh Percy, a brigadier under his command, to keep secret the expedition to Concord, and when Percy told him that the secret was out, Gage exclaimed that he had been betrayed, adding that he had communicated his design to one person only besides his lordship. According to gossip the "one person" was the general's wife, who informed the Americans.

The night before had been restless and disquieting for the Minutemen in nearby Lexington. Dr. Joseph Warren had discovered the British plot and on April 18 had sent Paul Revere, the leading New England silversmith, by way of Charlestown, and William Dawes via Roxbury, to spread the alarm. Revere galloped toward Lexington shouting the news to every house he passed.

Revere remembered: "The moon shone bright. I had got almost over to Charlestown Common towards Cambridge when I saw two [British] officers on horseback. . . . I turned my horse about, and rid upon a full gallop for Mistick Road." "In this brief, slippery cross-country race the heavier British charger . . . was no match for the lightfooted Yankee horse."[1] When he reached the house of the Rev. Jonas Clark in Lexington, where Adams and Hancock were staying, he found the place guarded by eight Minutemen, who warned him to make no noise lest he disturb the inmates. "Noise!" cried Revere. "You'll soon have noise enough, the regulars are coming!" However, Paul Revere did not escape later capture, but he was soon released.

The Minutemen at Lexington were under the command of Captain John Parker, veteran of the French and Indian Wars, who directed the sixteen-year-old William Diamond to beat the call to

1. From *Paul Revere and the World He Lived In* by Esther Forbes. Boston: Houghton, Mifflin Co., 1942.

arms. When Diamond enthusiastically rolled his drum at dawn on April 19, the War of the American Revolution had begun. Sam Adams, upon getting news of this, exclaimed to Hancock: "Oh, what a glorious morning is this!"—an impassioned observation which fell flat, since Hancock apparently thought his companion was referring to the weather. The two men promptly left the scene and so escaped capture.

The seventy Americans stood on the village common, their guns primed, as several hundred British troops marched up the road. Their position was ridiculously exposed and Parker was fully aware that his men could have found good cover in the nearby woods. But if the enemy opened fire, he wished, as did the colonial leaders in Massachusetts, the assault to look as bad as possible for the British and make every American colonist realize that life under the rule of the Crown was impossible.

Parker lined up his men as Major John Pitcairn of the British Marines approached the group. He commanded them, "Stand your ground. Don't fire, but if they mean to have a war, let it begin here." Pitcairn ordered his men likewise, telling them to surround the Americans and disarm them. At that point, in the tenseness of the moment, "a report from an unidentified firearm brought . . . a series of volleys from the British platoons."[2] This started the battle, with Pitcairn riding among his men shouting orders to stop firing. But what had begun could not be stopped.

Most of Parker's men dispersed, leaving eight dead and ten wounded, while only one British soldier was wounded. Lexington was less a battle than a hysterical massacre.

Later in the morning Parker reassembled his detachment and marched toward Concord to the beat of William Diamond's drum. "And this was perhaps Lexington's saddest and most triumphant moment—the sun now high in the sky, the smell of British gunpow-

2. From *Encyclopedia of American History,* edited by Richard B. Morris. New York: Harper & Row, 1965.

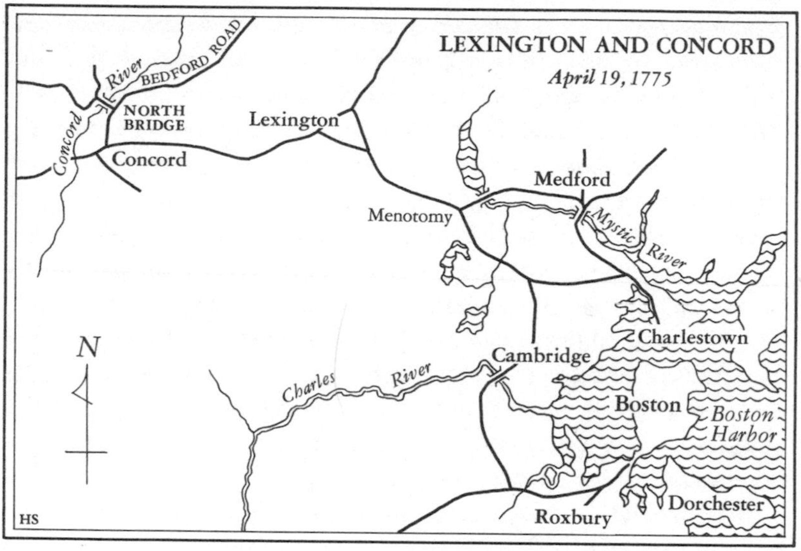
LEXINGTON AND CONCORD
April 19, 1775
BEDFORD ROAD
Concord River
NORTH BRIDGE
Concord
Lexington
Menotomy
Medford
Mystic River
Charlestown
Cambridge
Charles River
Boston
Boston Harbor
Roxbury
Dorchester
N
HS

der still in the air, their dead brothers lying on the Common behind, and the company of minutemen, knowing what they faced, marching off to meet the enemy again."[3]

At this time the population of Concord amounted to fifteen hundred people and included a number of Tories. At daybreak on April 19 a scout had been sent out from the town; he reported what had taken place at Lexington, and upon this intelligence, two hundred and fifty Minutemen under Major Buttrick assembled for a council of war. As a result of this conference, held in an atmosphere of complete calm, the three companies fell in line and marched down the road toward Lexington, the drums and fifes playing "To Meet the British."

Amos Barrett, one of the Minutemen, reported: "We marched

3. From *William Diamond's Drum* by Arthur B. Tourtellot. New York: Doubleday & Co., 1959.

down toward Lexington about a mile and a half, and we saw them coming. We halted and stayed until they got within about one hundred rods." Then Buttrick's force executed an about-face as the opposing forces met, and preceded the seven hundred British soldiers with all fifes and drums playing, marching toward Concord.

When the British reached Concord, they found that most of the military stores had been hidden—fortunately, for if the powder had been seized, it would have been a severe blow to the colonists. Seven companies of their light infantry occupied the North Bridge near the town while, on a hill two hundred yards away, the whole strength of four hundred provincial militia was established. There they held another conference as they saw smoke rising from the village; apparently the British were setting fire to the town, where many of the militiamen had left their families. The group agreed to march over the bridge, under strict orders not to fire until the enemy guarding the bridge did so. This column was the first American "army" ever to take the field.

The British opened fire, upon which Major Buttrick gave the order: "Fire, fellow soldiers, for God's sake, fire!" At this volley the British turned and ran toward Concord. But after forcing the bridge and sending the enemy in full retreat, and after isolating three other companies on the far side of the river, the Americans failed to press their advantage. They no longer were a unified force; with the casualness and independence that were to characterize the colonials and that persisted even under Washington's leadership, the Americans wandered off in different directions—not so much abandoning the fight as going their own way.

Back in Concord, at noon, the British nursed their wounded. The redcoats, infuriated by the Americans' "dirty fighting" (firing from behind rocks and trees in contrast to their exposed formation at Lexington), rushed from house to house, killing as they retreated from the town. Colonel Francis Smith and Major Pitcairn dreaded the prospect of marching back to Boston through enemy territory; their troops started limping toward Lexington, at first meeting with

no resistance. Then, at Meriam's Corner, a mile from Concord, they were met by the colonials and, as they passed over a narrow bridge, the Minutemen opened a devastating fire. At first the British stood and returned the fire, but soon started to panic. As they ran into the hail of enemy bullets, they realized that they still had fifteen miles to go before reaching Boston. One of their officers estimated that five thousand colonials were now swarming along both sides of the road; actually there were nowhere near that many, although the woods seemed full of Minutemen firing from behind rocks and trees, taking effective cover. The Minutemen converted houses along the road into miniature fortresses; in clearing them the enemy was forced into hand-to-hand fighting. It was a nightmare for the British, who were fighting bravely, but, just before reaching Lexington, their morale collapsed. They had become a running mob. In the retreat from Concord the British losses were three times as great as those of the Americans.

The end seemed inevitable for the retreating troops, when, at Lexington, a four-pound cannon ball, fired from a British field piece, crashed through a building. This was the first artillery fire of the day and was directed by Hugh Percy. "I had the happiness of saving them [the retreating British] from inevitable destruction," he wrote to his father, the Duke of Northumberland. Percy formed his men into a hollow square, enclosing the exhausted, fleeing regulars, who fell on the ground "with their tongues hanging out of their mouths like those of dogs after a chase," reported a British officer. He held up the pursuit for an hour and gave the tired men a respite and a chance to eat.

When the British finally reached Charlestown, on the outskirts of Boston, under the welcome shelter of their fleet, they were a routed mob. They had lost 273 men as against American losses of 93. The day's fighting had proved the worth of the town system of organized militia, whose uncertain aim was aided by their possession of some rifles that were more effective than the smooth-bore muskets used by the enemy.

Lord Percy, at the end of this historic day, expressed admiration for the provincial troops and prophesied: "Whoever looks upon them as an irregular mob will find himself much mistaken; they have men among them who know very well what they are about, having been employed as rangers against the Indians and Canadians, and this country being much covered with woods and hills, is very advantageous for their method of fighting." He might have added that the phenomenon of a whole countryside in arms made the British hesitant to march through enemy territory.

Except for Percy's decisive artillery action the British had shown little skill in fighting. As for the colonials, they could—by better coordination—have destroyed most of the enemy before Percy opened fire. That Lexington and Concord had been vitally helpful to the colonials there can be no question; these skirmishes resulted in the British Army's being cooped up in Boston, whither the colonial Tories fled. Besides, the event itself was backed by effective propaganda directed from Massachusetts, claiming that the British had fired first at Lexington and that they had destroyed property. Irresolution vanished within fourteen hours and the idea of reconciliation with the Crown was abandoned in Massachusetts.

It had been a tense day for the colonials and a tragic one for many of their families; it was also a day of commitment, for they had all been guilty of high treason against the King. The Provincial Congress, the creation of Sam Adams, had been the guiding force behind the fighting; it derived its strength from the succession of town meetings. These town fathers were thinking deeply about the implications of Lexington and Concord.

The arrival of Joseph Warren on the scene brought confidence. To the conglomeration of militia that were pouring in, northwest of Lexington, Warren represented the Committee of Safety and was the only commander they knew. It was Warren who primarily inspired the propaganda to the colonies and, although he was a truthful, honorable man, his statements—distorted, as happens in every war —told of horrors that never took place.

The Committee of Safety, with Warren as chairman, now had its army numbering twenty thousand, but it consisted of men who simply felt bound "to meet the British" and who had no idea of engaging in a long campaign. "Milling around Cambridge they were almost wholly unorganized. While some had a company structure, with elected officers to whom they gave little authority, others joined in little groups with every man his own general. They would stay as long as they saw fit and go home again."[4]

Back in Lexington the townspeople followed through on what they had started; in May Captain Parker mustered forty-five men, marching them to Cambridge to help in the siege of Boston. A month later, he took sixty-four to take part in the Battle of Bunker Hill; three months later he was dead from advanced tuberculosis. The record of the men of Lexington was remarkable; after the provincial militia had become part of the Continental Army 106 men enlisted out of a population of 750. For six years they were either chased by the British or followed them all the way down to Yorktown. Among them was William Diamond, who grew up in the army, returned to Lexington after the war, married and had six children.

From Lexington came heroes.

4. *Ibid.*

IX

The Fateful
Summer of 1775

THE BATTLE AT LEXINGTON widened the breach with England.
Even then, in the spring of 1775, Sam Adams stood almost alone in
the Second Continental Congress for wishing independence, the
majority being far from ready to advocate it at that time. The battle
was still a local quarrel between the people of Massachusetts Bay
province and Gage's troops occupying Boston; there existed no
united colonial authority behind the militia around Cambridge. The
Massachusetts delegation to the Second Continental Congress saw its
mission: to establish a national army, to stop conciliation efforts by
the other colonies, to make the cause of Massachusetts that of all the
colonies, and to make this clear to foreign countries. Without Lexington and Concord these objectives would have been impossible of
achievement.

The date set for this Congress was May 10, 1775, in Philadelphia.

The Massachusetts delegates, John and Samuel Adams, Robert Treat Paine and John Hancock, prepared for the journey. Sam could not ride a horse; this distressed John, who believed horsemanship essential "to the character of a statesman." Within a few days Sam mastered the art, and when the travelers reached Philadelphia, John heard it said that his cousin rode 50 percent better than he!

Sam and Hancock—an odd pair—traveled together for part of the journey. Hancock was vain and dressed elaborately; in contrast Adams normally wore shabby clothes, stained as well. For this occasion, however, his friends had put up money to outfit him properly. So he looked resplendent in new suit, wig and cocked hat, and a gold-headed cane.

It was typical of Hancock's overweening vanity that he became infuriated when, at Worcester, no reception committee welcomed him. He thereupon wrote a blistering letter of protest to the Provincial Congress at Watertown.

At Hartford Sam and Hancock conferred with Governor Jonathan Trumbull of Connecticut. Adams stated his conviction that the first strategic move of the British would be to attempt to split the colonies by sending an army through Lake Champlain and down the Hudson to New York City and so isolate New England from the West and South. Anticipating this, Adams had sent John Brown, a member of the Provincial Congress, to Canada to assess Canadian public opinion as well as the conditions of the old forts which had been garrisoned at the end of the French and Indian Wars. Brown reported that the fort at Ticonderoga "must be seized, as soon as possible, should hostilities be committed by the King's Troops."

Upon receipt of this report the Massachusetts Committee of Safety appointed Benedict Arnold to attack Ticonderoga. He set out from Connecticut and, at Castleton, Vermont, met with Ethan Allen and his Green Mountain Boys, who had been sent by the Connecticut Committee of Safety. The two of them disputed as to which should be in command—Arnold had the authorization, but Allen had the men. They settled their quarrel by agreeing to storm the fort to-

gether and did so with two boatloads carrying eighty-three militiamen. When the Green Mountain Boys reached Ticonderoga, all the
defenders were asleep except for one sentry, who promptly ran
away. Arnold, having gained access to the inside of the fort, wished
to act with dignity, but this presented a problem since Ethan Allen
was already brandishing his sword and shouting at the door of the
British commanding officer: "Come out, you old rat!" On May 9,
1775, the fort was captured without a shot having been fired.

So, on the day before the Second Continental Congress met, the
first American offensive occurred at a wilderness spot near Lake
George.

Sam Adams and Hancock continued their journey to Philadelphia
and in New York received a great ovation, which Hancock attributed entirely to himself. His hypocritical comment is a classic of
pompous self-adulation: "When I got within a mile of the city my
carriage [no mention of Sam, who was beside him] was stopped and
persons appearing with proper harnesses insisted upon taking out my
horses and dragging me into and through the city, a circumstance I
would not have had take place upon any consideration, not being
fond of such parade. They were at last prevailed upon [to desist] and
I proceeded; in short no person could possibly be more noticed than
myself."

In the six following paragraphs of this letter, each more nauseating
than the preceding, not a word is written about the real significance
of the reception, nor a word about Lexington and Concord.

Another traveler to Philadelphia, John Adams, took a dim view
of New York. He wrote: "With all the opulence and splendor of the
city there is very little good breeding to be found—I have not seen
one real gentleman, one well bred man, since I came to town."[1]

The delegates to the Continental Congress convened in the Pennsylvania State House. Though this Congress had no more validity

1. From *The Adams Family* by James Truslow Adams. Boston: Little, Brown, 1930.

than the provincial ones, and its delegates had no uniform authority, the meeting was a momentous occasion.[2]

The idea of separation from the mother country was still painful to most delegates, who felt that one more attempt should be made to reach an understanding. They resolved upon a petition to the King and, knowing George's violent opposition to dealing with the colonies as a united body, tactfully signed their petitions severally— as individuals speaking for the people. To evidence their concilia- tory mood, they entrusted the petition to Richard Penn, a descend- ant of the great Quaker, William Penn. He arrived in London in mid-August, but the King refused to see him or to receive the petition; to George the Congress was an illegal body. He forthwith issued a proclamation calling upon all loyal subjects of the realm to bring to punishment the leaders of the foul treason shown by the American colonies.

George III's next move was to ask Catherine of Russia for twenty thousand men, since "loyal subjects of the realm" had been slow to volunteer because the war was unpopular in England. Catherine indignantly refused to sacrifice her men's lives for pay and asked George if he thought it dignified to employ foreign troops against his own subjects.

The King, who was Elector of Hanover, then applied to the rulers of several German duchies, among them Hesse-Kassel and Hesse- Hanau, and obtained twenty thousand of the finest infantry in Europe as well as four good generals. Although this action was bitterly attacked by Liberals in Parliament, the Germans set sail, having no choice but to obey their rulers. The German people were indignant, and Frederick the Great wrote Voltaire that he was dis- gusted. He immediately levied a toll on all Hessians who passed through Prussian territory—"as upon cattle exported for foreign

---

2. A few blocks away from where the Congress met hundreds of ragged colonists were filing into Philadelphia's poorhouse not long before Thomas Jefferson was declaring it "to be self-evident, that all men are created equal."

shambles." Nevertheless, Frederick did permit these mercenary troops to cross his territory and so aided the British war effort. His performance, in this instance, was hypocritical.

In the autumn Parliament took the same rigid position on the American problem as it had previously, despite those members who urged a reasonable approach. Truculent Lord Germain took over American affairs and colonial resentment was aroused when Captain Henry Mowat sailed into Portland harbor (now Falmouth), setting fire to the town with shells and grenades, burning three-quarters of the buildings to the ground and turning out of doors a hundred men, women and children as winter approached.[3]

When news of this and of the hiring of Hessians reached Philadelphia, the delegates were outraged so that the group in favor of temporizing was reduced to a helpless minority. The Congress urged South Carolina to seize British vessels in their waters, adopted the plan, already being implemented, for expelling the enemy from Canada, and appointed a committee to deal with foreign powers.

The work of this committee bore fruit: in March of 1776 Louis XVI ordered one million livres of munitions to be supplied to the colonies, and Charles III of Spain sent the same kind of help shortly thereafter. From these sources the colonies received 80 percent of their gunpowder in 1776 and 1777. The French connection was formalized in February of 1778 when the Franco-American Alliance was signed.

As Samuel Adams was attending the Congress in mid-May of 1775, he was lost in melancholy reflection; he was big enough to realize that, while highly effective as an agitator, mob manipulator and politician, he had limitations as a statesman. He saw that the task ahead in the Congress would demand high statesmanship, particularly because the suspicion of Massachusetts ran so deep that even Lexington could not change it. Such thoughts troubled him.

3. This action was officially disavowed by the British government.

Sam's cousin John, on the other hand, suffered from no such melancholy reflections. Thirteen years younger than Sam, he had an intellectual cast of mind that could not conceive of any solution to a problem save through reason. John Adams came to Philadelphia with zest for the intellectual exercise in the sessions of the Congress, while Sam approached them with reluctance.

"John Adams wrote in his diary an entire program for the Second Continental Congress: 'I thought the first step ought to be to recommend to the people . . . to seize on all the Crown officers, and hold them with civility, humanity, and generosity, as hostages for the security of the people of Boston and to be exchanged for them as soon as the British army would release them [this was unnecessary, because—then unknown to Adams—Gage permitted inhabitants who wished to do so to leave Boston]; that we ought to recommend to people of all the States to institute governments for themselves, under their own authority, and that without loss of time; that we ought to declare the Colonies free, sovereign and independent states, and then to inform Great Britain we were willing to enter into negotiations with them for the redress of all grievances and a restoration of harmony between the two countries, upon permanent principles. All this I thought might be done before we entered into any connections, alliances or negotiations with foreign powers. I was also for informing Great Britain very frankly that hitherto we were free; but, if the war should be continued, we were determined to seek alliances with France, Spain and any other power of Europe that would contract with us. That we ought immediately to adopt the army in Cambridge as a continental army, to appoint a General and all other officers, take upon ourselves the pay, subsistence, clothing, armor and munitions of the troops.' "[4]

John Adams's opinions were too extreme for many of the delegates, and a deep chasm existed especially between the New England point of view and that of the Southern states; the egalitarian

4. From *William Diamond's Drum, op. cit.*

practices of the Northeast militia were abhorrent to the romantic Southerners with their fixation about an officer class. Beyond that the Congress was far from united, for many of the delegates had serious doubts about independence, which only Sam and John Adams and Franklin advocated. In Virginia, for example, the ties with England were strongly emotional; there the Church of England was entrenched and the landed aristocracy was attached to ceremony. In New York, too, the Church of England was the established one, while in Pennsylvania men of the Quaker faith disapproved of the militancy in Massachusetts. In addition, there was a clash of economic interests between the commercial North and the agrarian South. The representatives of the majority of the colonies feared the establishment of a nation run by Boston zealots, concerned equally with God and with the shilling. So it is not surprising that many feared that, were the authority of the Crown removed, the country would be in for a succession of internecine quarrels and even wars.

During the first three days of the Congress the time was spent reading the Lexington depositions, fixing the blame on the British and memorializing the Ministry in London. The Massachusetts delegation officially requested that the Congress take over the army "by appointing a generalissimo"; Sam Adams urged that the capture of Ticonderoga be used as the point of departure for an invasion of Canada.

The sessions droned on as the hot May days passed, and John Adams fumed at the lack of accomplishment. Especially galling to him was the conservative faction led by John Dickinson of Pennsylvania, who on July 5, 1775, introduced the ill-fated resolution petitioning the King for negotiations which might lead to reconciliation. Adams spoke vehemently in opposition, after which Dickinson followed him into the courtyard and told him that "if the New Englanders don't concur with us in our pacific system, a number of us will break off from you in the Northeast and we will carry on the opposition ourselves in our own way." Though this was very hard for John Adams to take, he was determined not to walk into a trap that would fatally divide the Congress. Accordingly he forced himself to vote for Dickinson's resolution.

The Congress had voted for John Hancock as president; the position carried with it no real authority and, at all events, there's no evidence that he showed any kind of leadership. In contrast to Hancock, Dr. Joseph Warren *did* show leadership. The communication he had sent from the Massachusetts Provincial Congress to the Continental Congress not having been delivered, Warren dispatched another through Dr. Benjamin Church, one of the members of the Massachusetts Congress. Church, a highly dubious Patriot, thereupon wrote a polite note to General Gage explaining that he could not do any spying for him for a while, on account of the journey he was obliged to take to Philadelphia! Dr. Church did deliver Warren's message and hung around Philadelphia for a while in the hope of picking up information that would be useful to Gage. The Congress, when informed about Church's treasonable behavior, was stupefied. John Adams wrote: "At the story of the Surgeon General [Church], I stand astonished. A man of genius, of learning . . . a writer of Liberty Songs . . . a speaker of Liberty Orations, a Member of the Boston Committee of Correspondence . . . good God! What shall we say of human Nature?"

The letter from Massachusetts, bearing Dr. Warren's stamp, had been carefully prepared; it urged self-government for the colonies, thereby advocating the *de facto* end of British rule and the need to create a Continental Army. Furthermore, it implied that Massachusetts could not, and would not, set up a permanent civil government without the consent of the Continental Congress; this forced upon the Congress the role of central authority over all the colonies. Finally, by urging the Congress to take over the army assembling at Cambridge, the petition placed the civil authority over the military.

Unfortunately, Congress appeared unwilling to act; many delegates still hoped for a peaceable word from England. On Friday, June 2, Hancock read the Massachusetts petition and John Adams immediately spoke strongly for its adoption, arguing that all the colonies should institute new governments. He was light-years ahead of almost all his fellow delegates, who were still trying to find ways of living harmoniously with the British. As a result of Adams's brilliant oration the Congress tabled the Massachusetts petition rather than turning it down.

On the next day the matter was considered again and a committee of five—not one of them from the Northeast—was appointed to consider the petition. John Adams and his supporters must have felt utterly discouraged, although, surprisingly, Sam seemed relaxed and observed: "The spirit of patriotism prevails among the members of Congress but, from the necessity of things, business must go slower than one would wish. It is difficult to possess upwards of sixty gentlemen at once with the same feelings upon questions of importance that are continually arising."

At last, on June 7, Congress recognized the right of the people to set up their own government and to ignore a tyrannical one, but it avoided accommodating Massachusetts with any advice or consent to the establishment of a "permanent" government. Nevertheless, this was a big step forward considering that the Congress was still expressing loyalty to the King. In advising a colony to establish its own government Congress set itself up, *ipso facto,* as the central authority within the colonies. Still unsolved was the question of adopting the Northeast army—a very thorny one since to have done so would have meant the commitment of all the colonies to war with England.

Actually, the idea of the Revolution was unpopular in America. Had the colonists anticipated the length of the war, they would have forced the Continental Congress to end it in 1776. And had the British government understood the tenacity of George Washington or foreseen the entry of France, Spain and Holland into the war, it might have conceded everything Congress demanded.

The key to the adoption by Congress of the Northeast army was the appointment of a commander-in-chief. John Adams was the only member prepared to press this, for his cousin Sam distrusted military authority and favored the appointment of officers by the Minutemen —and Adams's other colleagues from Massachusetts were of no help. As might be expected, John Hancock considered that *he* would make the perfect commander-in-chief. Cushing's choice was for a New Englander; Paine favored his college mate, Artemas Ward; while John Adams felt strongly that, in order to offset the anti-New England prejudice, the commander should come from the South. He had spotted George Washington in uniform among the delegates, had been struck by his dignity and quiet bearing; in addition, he had been impressed by Washington's patriotism—revealed by this soldier's resolution to raise and personally pay for a force of a thousand men to lift the siege of Boston. John Adams was determined to push for the appointment of Washington as commander-in-chief, a move Sam only reluctantly endorsed. In the Congress there were many superior to Washington in learning and eloquence, but Patrick Henry said of him: "If you speak of solid information and sound judgement, Colonel Washington is unquestionably the greatest man upon that floor."

John went to work in his dogged way, buttonholing delegates outside the State House. With Cushing and Paine he got nowhere and, of course, could not mention Washington's name to Hancock. From representatives of other colonies came objections—Washington's military ability was unproven, they said. And when Adams brought up the subject of Washington's service in the French and Indian Wars, his attention was called to the fact that every engagement in which Washington participated had been lost.[5] Nevertheless, Adams pressed on, despite adverse views from Washington's fellow delegates from Virginia.

On Wednesday, June 14, Adams made his nomination for the commander-in-chief of the Continental Army. In eloquent phrases he described the qualities needed for the ideal commander, "who was among us and very well known to all of us, a gentleman whose

5. He did win one—the "Jumonville Affair."

skill and experience as an oficer, whose independence of fortune, great talents and excellent universal character would command the approbation of all Americans and unite the cordial exertions of all the colonies better than any other person.

John Hancock was delighted and not surprised to hear these words since it was obvious to him that no one be he himself combined all such superlative qualities. He beamed upon the assembled delegates and was doubtless preparing his acceptance speech when Adams, completing his presentation, loudly declaimed the name of George Washington. The nomination was seconded by Sam, but John was alarmed when several delegates leaped to their feet in opposition. Various candidates were put forward and, at the end of the day's session, no decision had been reached.

However, nothing could long discourage John Adams in taking an action upon which he had decided; he spent the evening persuading delegates, feeling that those who had not spoken were for Washington.

On the following morning Thomas Johnson of Maryland renominated Washington, with the astonishing and momentous result that he was unanimously elected. That day, June 15, 1775, eight weeks after young Diamond had beat his drum, marked an important milestone in the War of Independence.

John Adams had succeeded in his important design of making the New England army into a Continental one with a commander-in-chief generally acceptable to the country; he thus made a vital contribution to the Second Continental Congress. But, though a much abler statesman than Sam, he lacked his cousin's genius for manipulating the delegates and public opinion. John often acted on the premise that "public opinion be damned." So, naturally, he reacted violently to John Dickinson's proposal that New England be allowed to go its own way while Pennsylvania and the Southern colonies would find accommodation with the mother country. Sam, on the contrary, had been unwilling to oppose Dickinson's petition to the King, being sufficiently well informed about British politics at the time to know that, like the previous one, it would be rejected. He realized that, unless the petition were made and then turned down by the British, Pennsylvania and the middle colonies would refuse to consider independence.

The two Adamses were in interesting contrast: John, a master theoretician, who nevertheless displayed his emotions; Sam, a passionate but severely disciplined person with a single purpose, who knew just when and how to conciliate.

X

Bunker Hill

DURING THE SESSION AT PHILADELPHIA colonial forces were sur-
rounding Boston in a semicircle sixteen miles long; the place qua-
lified as a peninsula, but its sole tie to the mainland was Boston Neck
—a mile-long causeway. The Americans numbered seven thousand;
the British, four. The colonials, commanded by Artemas Ward, had
plenty of spirit but little discipline—and they were poorly equipped.

General Gage despised the American troops, made bold statements, but hesitated to make any move. He and the British military,
and officials, seemed to have no idea what they were up against. In
the latter part of 1773, Gage, then commander-in-chief in America,
had gone to England to advise a show of force "against which they
[the Bostonians] would undoubtedly prove very weak." It was
Gage, nicknamed "Old Woman" by his own men, who was weak,
blustering to put up a front. The only justification for his appoint-

ment was that, at a moment when passions were running high, a conciliatory general had his uses. Nevertheless, Gage was deeply resented by the colonists, in spite of the fact that they still remained loyal to the King.

Another British soldier, General John A. Grant, misjudged the military capacity of the colonists. He announced that with a thousand soldiers "he would undertake to go from one end of America to the other, and geld all the males, partly by force and partly by a little coaxing."[1] He was to learn differently after facing Washington in New Jersey.

When General Gage learned that Lord North's efforts at conciliation had collapsed, he felt that he must take the initiative. His military position was poor and his fighting spirit negligible, but he was cheered by the arrival of the *Cerberus* with three major generals— William Howe, Henry Clinton and John Burgoyne. Hailing a ship as they entered the harbor, the generals learned that their army was encircled by the rebels. "What," cried Burgoyne, "ten thousand peasants keep four thousand King's troops shut up! Well, let *us* get in, we'll soon find elbow room!" Thus Burgoyne earned his nickname, "Elbow Room."

Gage realized that if the Americans seized Dorchester Heights to the south of the city or those of Charlestown across the Bay, Boston would become untenable. In June 1775, he held a council of war.

Sir William Howe was the senior of the three major generals. Up to the time of the Revolution his military record was excellent; he had served under Wolfe in the conquest of Canada and distinguished himself in the scaling of the Heights of Abraham, which effected the seizure of Quebec. But the Battle of Bunker Hill left a deep impression on him, and for the remainder of the war he shrank from making frontal assaults. Moreover, his strategy in the Revolution was not based on a clear conception of how the war might be won; in the eighteenth-century European military tradition he preferred

1. From *The American Nation* by John A. Garraty. New York: Harper & Row, 1966.

a war of posts and maneuver rather than a ruthless, single-minded pursuit of the Continental Army. In one particular he was wise: he did not underestimate the Americans but held them in high regard.

Sir Henry Clinton, while serving under Howe from 1776 to 1778, showed promise; but, once appointed commander-in-chief, he grew even more cautious and hesitant than Howe. In fact, he became a neurotic delayer.

"Burgoyne, a wit, bon vivant and playwright, has been pictured by some historians as a playboy who drank and danced his way to defeat. Actually, a hard driving, courageous commander consumed with ambition for fame, high rank and honor, he was a superb leader of men who recognized the role of ideology in the Revolutionary War and proved flexible enough to adapt his tactics to American conditions. At the same time he was hasty and seemed devoid of a sense of strategy."[2]

The British plans were discovered by American intelligence, and on June 15 the Committee of Safety directed its army to seize and fortify Bunker Hill on the Charlestown peninsula. General Artemas Ward and Joseph Warren, at a council of war, took issue with this directive, expressing a reluctance to move. They argued that their ammunition was low and that Bunker Hill was exposed to the guns of the British fleet. Major General Israel Putnam ("Old Put") disagreed vehemently, and he was rarely challenged.

On the night of June 16 he led twelve hundred men across Charlestown Neck. They dug in on Breed's Hill, the hill nearest to Boston.

Dressed mostly in homespun, dyed to match oak and sumac bark, the militiamen, each of whom owned his own equipment, for the most part carried old Brown Bess muskets from the colonial wars, with here and there an ancient Spanish fusee. "Old Put" rode ahead on a fine horse; beside him was Colonel William Prescott, a man as

2. From *George Washington's Opponents: British Generals and Admirals in the American Revolution,* edited by George A. Billias. New York: William Morrow & Co., 1969.

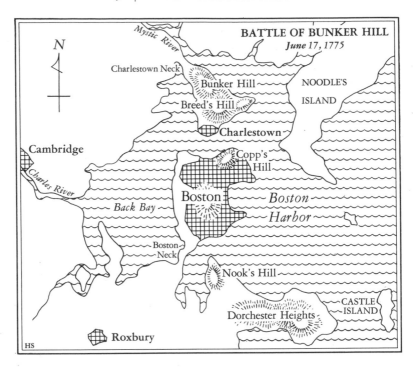

practical as Putnam was impetuous. Prescott was a fine, generous officer, and when he encountered Dr. Joseph Warren of Lexington before the battle, he saluted him as his superior officer, since Warren had just been appointed major general. Warren saluted back, saying: "I shall take no command here. I came as a volunteer with my musket to serve under you."

Prescott marched to Bunker Hill and thence to a ridge leading to Breed's Hill. The main fortification works were planned for Breed's, but Bunker Hill, which is 110 feet high, was fortified during the night as well, to cover a possible retreat. Having marked the lines of the redoubt, Prescott gave the command, "Dig!" His men obeyed with a will so that a British Marine sentry aboard the warship *Lively* stared, at sunrise, in disbelief at the red earth of the Yankee positions. The British fleet thereupon opened fire.

Meanwhile, the British generals discussed battle plans. It appeared that the one sure way to oust the colonials from Breed's Hill was to capture Charlestown Neck and cut off the enemy. But time seemed too precious, and it was decided to make a frontal assault on Breed before the Americans could plant on it a battery of siege guns which would threaten Boston. Another reason given for a frontal attack was "the general feeling [on the part of the British command] that it would be unmanly to catch the Americans in the trap which they had laid for themselves [!]. In a hasty Council of War it was decided to assault the redoubt in the good old British fashion of marching up its face."[3]

The British were certain that the "peasants" could not stand up to the assault of three thousand veterans. Gage, very confident, felt that in a few hours the disgrace of Lexington and Concord would be wiped out and the rebellion ended.

Because the tide was against them, the English could not land their men for six hours and the Americans took advantage of the delay. When the cannon balls smashed into them, Old Put, "in a rage of command,"[4] went everywhere along the line encouraging his men. Twice he rode across shot-swept Charlestown Neck calling urgently for reinforcements. Colonel John Stark responded to the call with his New Hampshire regiments; they were first-class sharpshooters but, unfortunately, had scarcely any ammunition.

At 1 P.M. twenty-two hundred redcoats under General Howe came ashore. On this day there was not a cloud in the sky and no battlefield could have been more spectacularly laid out, with the background of Boston's splendid harbor. As Howe paused to reconnoiter, Prescott used the time to improve his position. Then hell broke loose: Brigadier General Sir Robert Pigot was ordered to take

3. From *The Siege of Boston* by Allen French. New York: Macmillan Co., 1911.
4. From *The Wars of America* by Robert Leckie. New York: Harper & Row, 1968.

the redoubt while Howe attacked the breastwork.[5]

On the British left, American snipers in the houses of Charlestown whittled down the redcoats, who made an excellent target; the enemy ships in the harbor, as well as batteries planted on Copp's Hill in Boston, opened fire with red-hot ball and "carcasses"—hollow iron balls pierced with holes and filled with pitch. Charlestown became one great blaze.

Opposite Howe's main body, behind the breastwork, Old Put rode up and down the line, roaring: "Don't fire until you see the whites of their eyes! Then, fire low." Behind the Mystic River wall Colonel Stark went Putnam one better; he dashed forty yards ahead of the line, nailed a stake in the ground and yelled: "Not a man is to fire until the first regular crosses the stake." The British came on, sweating and suffering from the heat in their heavy uniforms and 120-pound packs; the Fusiliers swayed and went down, but the King's Own Regiment swept forward to fill the great rents in the attacking column. Another terrible volley from the Yankees sent the King's Own down in heaps, and now picked troops of the 3rd Regiment were ordered forward. Surely, they thought, the colonials could not fire a third volley so quickly—but they did, with devastating effect.

Still the redcoats came on; Howe pressed his men forward and two ranks, Grenadiers in front, came to the breastwork. The fire was murderous and every man on Howe's personal staff fell; but the general, who was in the forefront, remained untouched. He felt shamed that his trained troops lay "in heaps around him, shot down by ignorant peasants."

Again and again the British charged, suffering fearful losses. Things looked good for the Americans, and had not their staff work been poor, reinforcements of men and ammunition from Cambridge would have arrived and made a renewed British assault unsuccessful.

---

5. The British soldier, and presumably the American, could fire three rounds a minute; the best, five or six rounds. The powder in their guns was ignited with a flint.

The Battle of Bunker Hill

Unfortunately, as the Americans' ammunition began to run very low, the enemy had plenty, and had been reinforced. But the British command hesitated about mounting another costly attack, even as Prescott was preparing for a hand-to-hand encounter. Howe could, of course, still have attacked Charlestown Neck and cut off the Americans from the mainland, leaving them on the peninsula, where they would have been starved out. However, he could not endure the thought that his regulars would fail to dislodge the militiamen.

Finally, at 5 P.M. he mounted another assault. At first the advancing Britishers faltered under the savage American fire; then the militiamen's powder gave out. Yet they fought on, most of them without bayonets, using their guns as clubs, until Prescott shouted to them: "Give way, men! Save yourselves!" He then joined Putnam in directing the retreat, during which the Americans suffered most of their casualties. In the redoubt a British officer found a body, and from the quality of the dead man's ruffled shirt, he knew that this was a person of consequence. It was the gallant Joseph Warren. His modest heroism in refusing command and fighting to his death was typical of a day of noble deeds.

The Battle of Bunker Hill, during which the actual fighting lasted only an hour, was one of the costliest victories in British military annals; the English casualties were staggering. Of 2,400 engaged, 1,054 were shot, 226 fatally. The Americans suffered about 450 casualties, of which 140 were deaths. Although Howe suffered no wounds, his spirit was broken so that from a daring officer he turned slow and cautious. He failed to pursue the attack on the fleeing colonials and, although this may be attributed to his not wishing to achieve so complete a victory as to make a reconciliation impossible, the overriding reason was probably his own overcautiousness.

The Americans were elated after the battle and felt they had really won a victory, despite the final retreat. Thus was born the indestructible myth of the invincible Minutemen. Certainly they were steadfast and courageous at Bunker Hill, but, except for Stark's sharpshooters, Yankee marksmanship beyond point-blank range was poor—surprising in view of the fact that from the time of the first settlements able-bodied men in the colonies were required to bear arms because of the constant threat from the Indians. Besides, the colonists had been on call for military duty in the French and Indian Wars.

While the British blundered tactically, the Americans showed many shortcomings—lack of unified command, only a fifth of their forces having been brought into the action, and slowness in bringing up sufficient powder and reinforcements. And when the relieving troops did finally show up, many of them fled from the field of battle. At the end of the day Prescott was still unsupported; his men had been without food or water since early morning.

Moreover, the discipline of the militiamen was practically nonexistent and, in this connection, George Washington always excoriated the New England "leveling principle"—that every man is as good as the next, maybe a little better, making the enforcement of discipline a baffling problem. This lack of discipline was evidenced by the filthy state of the Yankee camps, which looked like hobo jungles.

Bunker Hill had great effect on public opinion both in the colonies and in Europe. While the British technically won the battle, London was incredulous that British troops had really been defeated by a crowd of "peasants." In contrast, the colonials felt that Bunker Hill was a moral victory, that they had demonstrated their ability to stand up against seasoned troops. Moreover, the battle made it possible for the Americans to continue their siege of Boston.

According to the British, the firing was hotter at Bunker Hill than anything they had previously known; and they considered the New England militiamen tougher than French regulars. Vergennes, the French Minister of Foreign Affairs, said that with two more such victories the British would have no army left in the colonies.

Bunker Hill encouraged George Washington, who felt that American liberties were now secure, while Franklin was of the opinion that Great Britain had lost the colonies forever. Such rosy views were not typical; even after the battle only the more hopeful citizens saw light ahead. Still lacking was any general sense of the colonies' real strength.

XI

George Washington Creates His Army

WHEN WASHINGTON WAS APPOINTED by the Continental Congress to head the Continental Army, he commanded the militia of Virginia with the rank of colonel. He was extremely reluctant to assume this great responsibility and felt inadequate for the assignment. James Flexner observes: "The traditional image of Washington presiding, during the Revolution, over a desperate cause with all the calm control of a marble statue is less accurate than would be an opposite vision: Washington plunging wildly from side to side, like an untamed bull in a restricted pen, trying to break the walls that hem him tight."[1]

He was forced into prominence too early. When given a position

1. From *George Washington in the American Revolution* by James Thomas Flexner. Boston: Little, Brown & Co., 1967.

of leadership in the French and Indian Wars at the age of twenty-two, he made a hasty attack which revealed his lack of experience.

Flexner makes this comment about Washington's subsequent career: "His path through the Revolution was studded with mistakes (from which he learned), indiscretions (which he repeated when the strain became again too strong), personal hatreds (few but powerful), boredom, resentments, lies, exaggerated complaints, and a great deal of personal misery. 'The poor general,' his wife observed, when he accepted command, 'was so unhappy that it distressed me exceedingly.' "[2]

Washington developed rare soundness of judgment and self-command over his strong emotions; he possessed the faculty of getting at the essentials of every problem. A civilian drawn by crisis from his farming pursuits, he disliked the military life and yet managed to outlast three British commanders-in-chief and to win a difficult war. Stately, but far from being a marble statue, he had a gay, informal side and was loved as well as admired by his associates.

Washington was fearless and once said: "I heard the bullets whistle and, believe me, there is something charming in the sound." Yet he was ready to bring on battle only when he thought the conditions were right. Perhaps his main strength as a military leader was sagacity rather than dash. He was an organizer, a chairman of councils of war, a coalition general somewhat on the model of that latter-day Virginian soldier, George C. Marshall. He kept things going for more than eight years, most of them bad years.

"He was . . . a natural leader but not an autocrat, a vigorous man but not a bully, an uncomplicated person but very far from stupid. We have learned to distrust hero worship. Yet in Washington's case the clichés nearly all seem to be true."[3]

2. *Ibid.*

3. From the biographical essay on Washington by Marcus Cunliffe in *The Harper Encyclopedia of American Biography,* edited by John A. Garraty and Jerome L. Sternstein. New York: Harper & Row, 1974.

The Continental Congress, in July 1775, directed Washington to proceed to Cambridge and take command of the troops there. He was appalled by what he saw: no unity of command, lack of discipline, no adequate commissary, lack of military supplies—and no money. Gradually, over several months, he created a fighting force and pried some funds out of a reluctant Congress.

The state of our so-called army at the time was graphically described by a surgeon of one of His Majesty's ships stationed in Boston: "My curiosity led me to make use of the privilege of my profession to visit the New England camp. . . . There is a large body of them [militiamen] in arms near the Town of Boston. Their camp and quarters are plentifully supplied with all sorts of provisions and the roads are crowded with carts and carriages, bringing them rum, cyder, etc. . . . for without rum a New England army could not be kept together; they could neither fight nor say their prayers, one with another. They drink at least a bottle of it, a man, a day.

"This army, of which you will hear so much said, and see so much more wrote about, is truly no more than a drunken, canting, lying, praying, hypocritical rabble. Without order, subjection, discipline or cleanliness, and must fall to pieces of itself in the course of three months."[4]

By degrees the Americans were made into good soldiers; without Washington it is doubtful whether this could have been achieved. He was up against great odds; when he took over the command from the aging Artemas Ward, he had less than fifteen thousand men, composed entirely of New Englanders. But within a few weeks three thousand arrived from Pennsylvania, Maryland and Virginia, including Daniel Morgan and his sharpshooters. Washington had little artillery and only sufficient powder to allot nine cartridges to each man in the event of an enemy attack. Most of the American officers, from colonel down, and all enlisted men, wore tattered clothes, not

4. From *The Spirit of 'Seventy-Six* by Henry Steele Commager and Richard B. Morris. New York: Harper & Row, 1967.

uniforms; the soldiers often had to fight in bare feet. Our army was so badly fed and clothed that Lafayette, de Kalb and von Steuben all stated that no European troops could have endured the hardships undergone by the Americans. In winter weather the colonial enlisted men lacked overcoats, a deficiency that was alleviated by the devotion of Patriot women, who went to work making coats for them. These women helped the cause in many ways; some took great risks as spies, others made much-needed munitions.

Whipping the colonial force into shape was indeed a problem. Although Washington discouraged some of the barbarous methods of enforcing discipline, he used corporal punishment and applied to Congress, unsuccessfully, for permission to administer one hundred lashes rather than the Biblical limit of thirty-nine, although in his heart he doubted the efficiency of punishment, feeling that troops were best improved by rigorous training.

Another of Washington's headaches was the need for constant recruiting. He was plunged into depression when only 3,500 men re-enlisted at the end of the year, leaving him with little more than half of the British force besieged in Boston. He wrote: "Such a dearth of public spirit, such stock jobbing—I never saw before and pray God's mercy I may never be witness to again." American soldiers believed in going home after the battle and, anyway, the early enlistments expired on January 1, 1776. Hence the achievement of a sizable, properly trained force was extraordinarily difficult.[5]

Washington also had to face the fact that each of the colonies was fielding an army of its own and that some of the Southern ones were reluctant to contribute troops to the Continental Army.

And there was disease to contend with. According to Dr. Richard B. Stark, Attending Surgeon at St. Luke's Hospital in New York

5. Based on the population of the colonies in 1776, roughly 2,600,000, a large army could have been raised—except for the problem of supplies. A force of 35,000 might have been sufficient to defeat the British without help from the French.

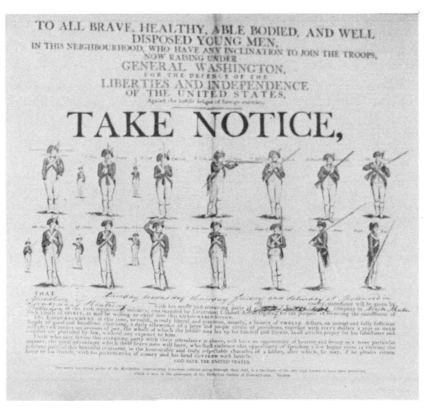

RECRUITING POSTER

City, "Disease accounted for much more morbidity and mortality than did British muskets. Smallpox, which defeated the American drive into Canada, spread to the Northern Department and soon became Washington's most formidable enemy." From the same source comes the astounding statement that at the end of 1776 Washington's "Grand Continental Army" had shrunk to 1,400; it had lost 1,200 wounded and 1,000 killed in that year—and 10,000 had died from disease!

Finally, there was the Negro problem. In the early days of the War, Congress barred their enlistment, but when Washington pointed out that they were joining the British side, tempted by the offer of their freedom, this ruling was reversed. In fact, many blacks fought in the Continental Army, thereby gaining their freedom.

One of the few heartening developments for the new commander-in-chief was that a number of able men volunteered as officers, notably, Henry Knox, Benedict Arnold, Nathanael Greene, and Daniel Morgan.

Morgan had made a big reputation in the Seven Years' War; he was a man of huge stature and great endurance. At Cambridge began Morgan's long friendship with young Benedict Arnold—a very different sort of character. Arnold was romantic and brave, but vain, self-seeking and without Morgan's moral strength.

Nathanael Greene, commander of the Rhode Island contingent, was a man of high intellectual caliber—he emerged from the war with a military reputation almost equal to that of Washington. And there was Henry Knox, the Boston bookseller, who was given command of the artillery. None of these younger officers had yet reached high rank, but they soon replaced the older, more senior officers. Major General Israel Putnam, a brave but militarily limited soldier, was an exception and remained in a high position for another year. All but one of these officers in Cambridge (Morgan was a Southerner) were New England men. Major General Philip Schuyler and Brigadier General Richard Montgomery of New York—both able—were now at Ticonderoga and the Indian frontier of New York.

There were two Englishmen at Cambridge—Horatio Gates, an imbecile intriguer, and Charles Lee; the latter had an estate in Virginia but was no relation of the illustrious Virginia Lees. A soldier of fortune, Lee had served the King of Poland and come to America when the war started—for the hell of it. He was loud and pompous of manner but impressed Americans with his enormous self-confidence. He hoped to be made commander-in-chief and therefore nourished a grudge against Washington, whose plans he later tried to thwart at a critical moment in the war. Lee was a bad lot.

Washington's army was a rabble. From the Cambridge Common to the river their rude tents were dotted around—some made of sailcloth stretched over poles, some of stones and turf, some of woven green boughs. No one knew how the soldiers were to be paid or fed; there was not at this time any government organized to support an army. It was amazing that they had subsisted for three months without any commissariat.

Until the end of the war Washington was harassed by lack of supplies. Little powder was made in the colonies and there was an acute shortage of weapons. The commander-in-chief tried his utmost to purchase weapons and, in desperation, considered the use of primitive implements as substitutes for muskets. The suggestion that the longbow be revived came from Franklin; this Washington turned down but said he would consider using pikes.

He could do with some encouragement at the end of 1775, for during December his army was melting away. Protests, like the one from General Charles Lee, were ineffective: "Men," he roared, after "entreating" them with curses and insults, "I don't know what to call you. You are the worst of all creatures." Washington lost his temper and wrote of the "dirty, mercenary spirit" of the men. But it must be realized that the men had enlisted for only eight months and that, while they served, their farms went uncared for or their trades were gobbled up by the stay-at-homes.

By January things had improved somewhat; of seven thousand men due to return to their homes nearly half re-enlisted. Also,

American privateers, organized by Washington, began to prey on British ships, seizing guns and ammunition.

Washington worried that the enemy in Boston, upon learning about the sad state of the Continental Army, would decide to take the offensive. They should have done so.

XII

The British
Evacuate Boston

IN THE FALL OF 1775 as the Second Continental Congress, for the first time representing all thirteen colonies,[1] was reconvening, the two opposing generals in Boston were ready for an attack, but neither was adequately prepared to make one. Howe was content to wait; Washington was not. On September 11 Washington had called a council of war proposing an attack on Boston; to this plan all his officers were opposed. A month later there was the same reaction at a staff meeting, except that General Greene disagreed. The officers kept emphasizing the shortage of powder—a secret that had been well kept from the British.

In October a committee of the Continental Congress, headed by Franklin, met with the commander-in-chief, his staff and delegates from the four New England colonies which, up to this time, had

1. Georgia had not previously participated.

mainly conducted the siege. Washington was encouraged by the progress that had been made in dissipating colonial jealousies, which had been such that General Greene felt obliged to assure the gentlemen from the southward "that the New England colonies, after conquering England, would not turn their arms to the South."

While Howe was struggling to survive the winter,[2] Washington was busy creating his army. A tall, elegant forty-three-year-old, he had been commander-in-chief for seven months since his arrival in Cambridge just after the Battle of Bunker Hill.

To the British, Washington was an enigma; they could not understand that a man of his caliber could be part of an illegal movement led by "riff raff like Sam Adams." They respected him, and it is significant that letters from British officers to Washington were phrased with elaborate courtesy.

Washington might have attacked at this time, and later regretted that he had not done so. The British were in as bad shape as the Americans, smallpox was plaguing them and food was short. The Ministry in London had shipped to Boston five thousand oxen, fourteen thousand sheep, quantities of hogs, vegetables, wood, coal, etc., but gales had wrecked some of the ships and others had been captured by the growing fleet of American privateers. Wood was scarce so that the soldiers stole it despite Howe's threat of death by hanging.[3] In the choice of houses to be chopped up for fuel, Patriots'

---

2. To fan discontent among the British soldiers in Boston, the colonials scattered handbills, when the wind was favorable, comparing conditions among American and enemy troops:

On Prospect Hill	On Bunker Hill
$7 a month	3 pence a day
Fresh provisions in plenty	Rotten salt pork
Health	The scurvy
Freedom, ease, affluence and a good farm	Slavery, beggary and want

From *The Siege of Boston, op cit.*

3. Or flogging. For this punishment soldiers were tied to a whipping post of crossed halberds and suffered 250 strokes administered by drummers wielding cat-o'-nine-tails. At the end of this torture salt water was poured on the bleeding lacerations to prevent infection.

Exposed to the Horrors of War, Pestilence and Famine, for a Farthing an Hour.

property was marked for destruction. Howe tried hard to maintain discipline\but not hard enough to forgo the charms of Betsey Loring, the American wife of the British commissary general.[4] His officers amused themselves too; the Old South Church was turned into a riding academy and plays, heretofore banned, were performed in Faneuil Hall. *The Blockade of Boston* burlesqued Washington and his ragtag army, and Washington was invited to attend the opening performance for the pleasure of watching himself being hanged. At this climax in the entertainment a sergeant rushed in, announcing, "The Yankees are attacking our works on Bunker's Hill." The English officers, who were dressed up as women for the play, heard the alarm and rushed from the scene in petticoats. What had happened was that Washington had sent a detachment to burn some houses in Charlestown. This had caused the cannonading.

Throughout that winter Howe believed that Washington was planning an attack, but although he kept Bunker Hill, to the north of Boston, fully manned, he left the Dorchester peninsula, to the south, unprotected, fearing to overextend his lines, already long in relation to his forces. However, Howe's decision made it possible for the Americans on the heights of Dorchester to repeat, precisely, the operation they had started on Bunker Hill and so make the city untenable for the enemy.

Washington took advantage of the situation and, having received a quantity of cannon from Ticonderoga, occupied Dorchester

---

4. In Philadelphia, two years later, the American Tories were exasperated with Howe's behavior and that of his officers, who gave themselves over to balls, horse racing and wine. One of them was so outraged at Howe's dalliance with Betsey Loring that he wrote this doggerel:

> Awake, arouse, Sir Billy,
> There's forage on the plain,
> Ah, leave your little filly,
> And open the campaign.

Footnotes 3 and 4 are from *The Wars of America, op. cit.*

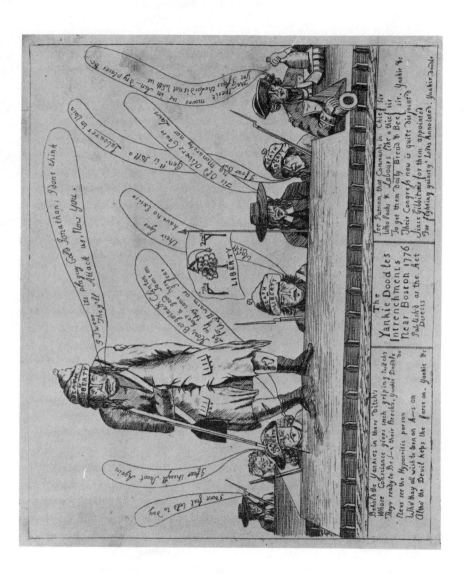

Heights during the night of March 4, 1776. Howe observed this but refused to be disturbed from his game of faro with Mrs. Loring. Early the next morning he realized the danger of his position and, when he viewed the American fortifications, observed, "The rebels have done more in one night than my whole army could have done in six months."

Howe ordered Lord Percy to assault the American works. At that moment a violent storm blew up and this persuaded the reluctant British command to delay attack. By dawn the following morning the American works on Dorchester Heights had been made impregnable; Percy's orders were countermanded and the decision was taken to abandon Boston. General Howe publicly announced that he was about to evacuate and threatened to burn the city if his troops were fired upon.

Had the storm not intervened, a decisive battle would have been fought. Washington had carefully planned a bold attack, although it probably depended too much on perfect timing. At all events, he was prepared to take great risks to achieve his aim of destroying the enemy force.

Washington could have cannonaded the departing enemy fleet but forbore to do so, and allowed the British to leave Boston unmolested. By March 17 eight thousand troops had been embarked, along with nine hundred Tory citizens. The British sailed away to their naval base at Halifax, leaving behind, in their haste, a huge quantity of military stores. They left a sad town; smallpox and lack of food had taken their toll, and the civilian population had fallen from seventeen thousand in 1774 to around three thousand.

So ended the long struggle for control of the key port of Boston; this was the last British defensive movement for a long time. As the ships sailed north, London was planning an attack to crush the rebels and end the Revolution. Strategic decisions were in the process of being transformed into action by an administration unequipped to handle a major operation. Nevertheless, their concept of a grand offensive was impressive:

A force of 9,000 for Sir Guy Carleton, royal governor of Canada, to relieve Quebec, clear Canada of Americans and attack from Lake Champlain, going down the Hudson

25,000 men to join Howe for an attack on New York by sea with the purpose of destroying Washington and his army

2,500 to sail for the South and form the nucleus of an army of Loyalists from Virginia and the Carolinas.

Grand on paper, but Lord George Germain, Secretary of State for the colonies, was faced with the graft-ridden Whitehall bureaucracy. He was responsible for supplying the largest force Britain had ever sent overseas—with tents, uniforms, food, muskets, cannon, etc.— and all was to be ready by late spring.

The time certainly seemed ripe for a declaration of independence. Continuing ambivalence in the colonies on this question was exemplified by a flag flown at Washington's headquarters in Cambridge on New Year's Day 1776. It consisted of thirteen stripes representing the united colonies, but, in the corner, the British crossed emblem remained!

Hastening the declaration was the King's action in hiring foreign troops to fight the colonists; feeling was running high when Thomas Paine's pamphlet *Common Sense* appeared in January 1776.

Paine, the English son of a corset maker, had arrived in America late in 1774. He needed work immediately, applied to Franklin for a job and was made editor of the Pennsylvania *Gazette*. Paine was a single-minded radical; his was not a subtle mind, but he had a great gift of expression. *Common Sense* swept the country—half a million copies of this fifty-page booklet were sold almost overnight. Actually it was pretty crude, offering as an argument a denial of the English origin of the colonies, but Paine's statement of the irreconcilable issue between the colonies and the King was compellingly eloquent; it was the right pamphlet at the right time.

A battle at Moores Creek in North Carolina on February 27, 1776, provided another powerful spur to declare independence. North Carolina was a prosperous community of planters, many of them Scots who had emigrated there from the western Highlands. George III counted on these Scots for support and had ordered Sir Henry Clinton to sail from Boston to North Carolina. At the same time Sir Peter Parker with seven regiments and ten ships of war sailed from Ireland to support Clinton. To complete the force the royal governor of North Carolina raised sixteen hundred men, who were to join Clinton.

As soon as the Patriots perceived this movement, a thousand Minutemen took their position at Moores Creek. Within half an hour the Scots were routed after a sharp fight; Captain Richard Caswell took nine hundred prisoners, £15,000 of gold and a quantity of arms.

The effect of this victory was contagious—like Lexington; within a few days ten thousand militia were raised to face Clinton, who then decided not to land his men. Sir Peter Parker and his troops did not show up until May.

North Carolina, forthwith, assembled a Provincial Congress which instructed their delegates to the Continental Congress "to concur with the delegates of other colonies in declaring independence."

Finally, on July Fourth, the Declaration of Independence was signed by John Hancock alone—an act of considerable courage since he was thus exposing himself to the wrath of the British government. It was "no mere political manifesto. As has been well said it is a kind of war song; it is a stately and passionate chant of human freedom; it is a prose lyric of civil and military heroism."[5]

Upon signing the Declaration in August with the rest of the signers, Samuel Adams ceased to be a key figure. The task ahead was to form an effective government, and, while Sam was unexcelled in overturning governments, he knew little about building them—and his knowledge of military matters was limited. After the Revolution

5. From *The Story of the Declaration of Independence* by Dumas Malone. New York: Oxford University Press, 1954.

CONGRESS VOTING INDEPENDENCE
(Engraving by Edward Savage after Robert Edge Pine and Edward Savage)

had started, his idea was to fight the British with state militia rather than with an enlisted regular army because he feared a military dictatorship. However, as the fighting went on and as he witnessed the general failure of the militia, his common sense asserted itself and he changed his mind.

Although Adams was ignorant about military affairs, he meddled with the War Department and backed the wrong generals, notably Charles Lee, whose abilities he considered far superior to those of George Washington. In 1777 Sam felt that Washington could have easily driven the enemy into the Atlantic and ended the war. But, in spite of proddings from Congress, Washington refused to risk his army in a decisive battle at the time, adopting instead the Fabian policy upon which his military reputation is based.

After Gates's victory at Saratoga, Adams wanted Washington to make way for General Gates. Sam had some important supporters —among them Richard Henry Lee and his cousin John; Gates himself was anxious for the post of commander-in-chief. When the plot to replace Washington failed—the plotters were known as the "Conway Cabal"—the cabal denied any attempt to throw Washington overboard.

Nevertheless, Adams's name was associated with the attempts to oust Washington and Sam's constant intriguing in Congress steadily diminished his standing among the Patriot colonists.

XIII

The Colonists
Invade Canada

WHILE THE COLONISTS speculated as to what Canada would do,
whether the Canadians would choose to throw off the British yoke,
Sam Adams acted; his agents had been moving through the area
urging the inhabitants to form Committees of Correspondence and
send delegates to Congress. His action contrasted with the cautious
attitude of Congress, which resolved on June 1, 1775, that no armed
expedition be sent to Canada. At the same time it discussed sending
a committee there to spread the gospel of freedom.

But when Benedict Arnold assured the members that Canada
would be quickly conquered and that he was the man to accomplish
it, Congress reversed itself. Ethan Allen, also, was in favor of invasion. The views of these two officers carried weight, and on June 27
Congress voted that "If General Philip Schuyler finds it practicable
and that it will not be disagreeable to the Canadians [!], he shall

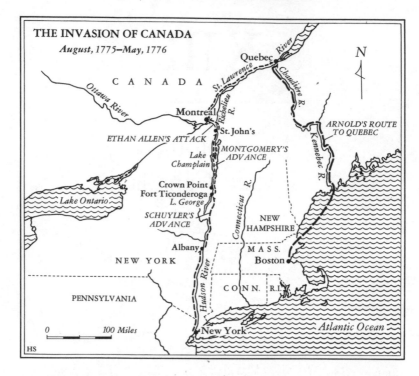

immediately take possession of St. John's, Montreal and any other parts of the country." Arnold and Allen seemed left out, but nothing could hold these men back; Allen soon joined Schuyler's forces at Crown Point and Arnold persuaded Washington to send him on a rival expedition through Maine and on to Quebec.

The conservative General Schuyler did consider the Canadian expedition practicable and proceeded to Ticonderoga for an offensive against Montreal. When Schuyler fell ill, the command passed to the resourceful young Richard Montgomery.

The Canadian invasion began when General Montgomery, on August 28, 1775, embarked about a thousand men on Lake Champlain. Sailing down the Richelieu he sighted the British fort of St. John's and there began his siege, which was slowed down by cold and rain. Thereupon, Ethan Allen with four hundred men, and his associate John Brown with two hundred, determined to capture Montreal. The initial attack failed, but St. John's finally fell and, shortly after, Montgomery received the capitulation of Montreal.

Meanwhile Benedict Arnold was advancing upon the old fortress at Quebec, going up the Kennebec River, with a thousand men, among whom served the nineteen-year-old Aaron Burr. The expedition ran into great difficulties: a hurricane struck in the wilderness; fatally delaying Arnold; the bateaux came apart in the rapids and men were drowned; provisions gave out so that the Americans had to eat soap and hair grease. They even boiled and roasted bullet pouches and leather breeches and devoured them. Such hazards appealed to the romantic Arnold, and he pressed ahead after two hundred of his men had succumbed to starvation, and another two hundred had given up and returned to Massachusetts.

On the black night of November 13 Arnold's men began crossing to the Anse-du-Foulon and, soon after, routed a British force on the Plains of Abraham. Arnold sent a flag of truce to Quebec demanding surrender, only to be driven off. Then, on December 2, Montgomery arrived on a schooner with three hundred troops and much-needed clothing. He and Arnold decided that to lay a long siege to Quebec was impossible—they lacked heavy guns and their men, riddled with smallpox, could not endure the Canadian winter. Accordingly, they agreed to attack once more, although Sir Guy Carleton, disguised as a farmer, had entered the city and raised the number of its defenders to eighteen hundred. Carleton, the royal governor, was a tubby, buoyant, energetic general who knew that he could do only little to challenge a major American attack. He had but a small force to protect the whole of Canada.

Snow began to fall in the afternoon of December 30. The following day at 4 P.M. the Americans attacked in a heavy blizzard; within Quebec the drums beat and the bells tolled. Arnold called for a charge against the ramparts and his men advanced as the enemy fired at them through the gunports. The assault nearly succeeded, but Arnold fell with a ball through his leg and the huge Daniel Morgan replaced him in command, climbing a ladder set against the barrier and urging his troops forward. Then a blaze of fire toppled him off the ladder, but he shook himself like a dog, reclimbed it and jumped over the parapet, his men close behind him. The defenders fled and the Americans were inside the Lower Town, where they awaited Montgomery and his forces, which arrived shortly but were confronted by a heavily fortified blockhouse. Though Montgomery came on, his men faltered. Through the storm he shouted, "Come on, my good soldiers, your general calls on you to come on." Within a few paces of the blockhouse Montgomery was hit and mortally wounded; the same fate befell most of his officers, and only Aaron Burr with a few others got away.

An able maneuver by Carleton had ended this attempt to storm Quebec. As time passed, more and more colonials were poured in, but the defenders held firm. In the spring a British fleet sailed up the St. Lawrence to raise the siege. It became blocked by twelve-foot ice and was stalled, when Captain Charles Douglas, commanding the fifty-gun ship *Isis,* decided to risk his naval career and break through. Two ships followed the *Isis,* and on May 6, 1776, the relief force sighted the towers of Quebec. The Americans were still encamped outside the town, but their morale was low and the troops were ravaged by smallpox.

Carleton, reinforced, attacked; the colonials retreated, abandoning Montreal as well.

"The attempt to conquer Canada, the most ambitious American expedition of the Revolutionary War, had ended in humiliating defeat."[1]

The repulse in Canada, shortly after the anniversary of Lexington, presaged a series of disastrous defeats for the colonists. The first

1. From *The Wars of America, op. cit.*

twelve months of the war had been surprisingly successful for the Americans, but during the years to come George Washington was kept on the run much of the time and, often, the colonial cause seemed lost.

Following the American withdrawal from Canada the colonials suffered defeat after defeat over five long years. Except for the part he played, along with the French Navy and Army, in the final British surrender at Yorktown in 1781, Washington achieved only a single clear-cut victory—the surprise attack on the Hessians at Trenton, New Jersey, followed by the capture of Princeton. Nevertheless, it was he who held the army together and maintained their spirit in the face of incredible hardships, as in the terrible winter at Valley Forge. He well deserved to be named a hero.

At the close of the Revolution the disunited colonies had achieved unity in their struggle for independence despite the occurrence of two mutinies among Washington's troops and a ghastly depreciation of the Continental currency. The stage was set for the creation of the American nation, but many carpenters were needed, for the solid front against the British often came apart when it was time to adopt the Constitution and establish a federal government. Moreover, while the Federal Constitution of 1788 marked an impressive advance for human rights, certain basic social reforms were still needed, such as universal suffrage to take the place of limited suffrage (often based on property qualifications) and equal rights for blacks.

It had been a long, hard war which neither side had wanted. In the course of it the American republican form of government evolved, with a profound, long-term effect upon the rest of the world, setting in train a whole series of revolutions of a different type from the American one: the French Revolution, those in nineteenth-century Latin America, the revolutions in Europe of 1848, the Russian Revolution of 1917, and the recent revolts in Asia and Africa. The American Revolution was remarkable in that it did not lead to a military or royal dictatorship.

Many dates have been set for the beginning of the modern age; 1775—the year of Lexington—may be the most meaningful, for not only did the American war establish the political climate for succeeding generations, but the machine age—the Industrial Revolution, which transformed the world—was then gathering momentum.

The roll of William Diamond's drum was more than a call to a handful of Minutemen; it announced the shape of things to come for the next two hundred years.

The Original Print done in England on the back of a Message Card, the Invention and for the use of BENJAMIN FRANKLIN ESQ; LL.D. Agent for the Province of Pennsylvania, in London.

XIV

Samuel Adams's
Last Years

DURING THE DARK DAYS of the war Sam Adams worked with his usual doggedness, but he failed to adapt himself to changing times. The singleness of purpose and fixity of mind that had made him so enormously effective as a radical leader proved a handicap in the end. He incurred the enmity of the Federalists by his opposition to the new Federal Constitution in 1787, to which he objected because it set up "a National government, instead of a Federal Union of Sovereign States." His weakness for government by committee, derived from his town meeting training, led a French Minister to lament over the man "whose obstinate, resolute character was so useful to the Revolution at its origin, but who shows himself so ill suited to the conduct of affairs in an organized government."

When he signed the Declaration of Independence, with that stroke of the pen he signed away his real vocation; it was the great, culminating point in his career, but this success ended his leadership. America no longer needed an agitator. His important work was done between 1765 and 1776; later he did serve as lieutenant governor of Massachusetts, becoming governor in 1794 when he succeeded John Hancock, but these were minor responsibilities in comparison with Adams's pre-eminence in earlier years. Nevertheless, his reputation abroad was immense. Two years after the Declaration of Independence when John Adams arrived in France, "he was asked if he was 'the famous' Adams . . . who had made himself the ruler of Congress. John protested that he was plain John Adams and not 'the famous' Adams."[1]

Sam Adams remained active in politics after the Revolution despite his waning influence. Having turned conservative in his old age, he denounced Shays' Rebellion, only to get back on his radical track when he sympathized with the French Revolution. And, when John Adams was feeling doubtful about the republican experiment in America, Sam believed that democracy would flourish provided the masses were educated. A sharp division took place at this time between the two Adamses—Sam, the Republican, believing in the Whig doctrine of states' rights and John, the Federalist, espousing a strong national government. They also differed sharply about the Jay Treaty of Peace, which Sam denounced as a sellout to Britain.

Before giving up his fight against federalism Sam determined on one last pitched battle. In 1796 John Adams was Federalist candidate for President to succeed George Washington, and Sam ran unsuccessfully as a presidential elector in Massachusetts opposing him. During John's campaign the candidate asked: "What is the reason that so many of our 'old standbys' are infected with [French] Jacobinism? The principles of this infernal tribe were surely no part of our ancient political creed."

Sam retired as governor and from public life in 1797. At last prosperous, due to a fortunate investment in Jamaica real estate,

1. From *Sam Adams: Pioneer in Propaganda, op. cit.*

Adams would sit on the doorstep of his yellow house or wander around his garden talking about old times. He lived to see Jefferson elected President and wrote him, "The Storm is over, and we are in port," when the Republicans assumed power.

As the years passed, Samuel Adams suffered from nervous disorders and this proud man became an object of compassion. On October 2, 1803, he died at the age of eighty-one. The bells tolled for half an hour, flags flew at half-mast, the president of Harvard joined the funeral procession to the Old Granary Burying Ground, where the body of the patriot was laid.

Adams's plot is marked by a boulder with a *modern* bronze plaque. In the *Pennsylvania Magazine of History* it was noted in 1880 that his burying place had been left unmarked: an example of the way the memory of Sam Adams has been neglected.

His most fitting epitaph would have been this entry in John Adams's diary: "Adams is zealous, ardent and keen in the cause, is always for softness and delicacy and prudence where they will do but staunch and stiff and strict and rigid and inflexible in the cause.—He is a man of refined policy, steadfast integrity, exquisite humanity, genteel erudition, obliging, engaging manners, real as well as professed piety—unless it should be admitted that he is too attentive to the public and not enough to himself and his family."

The Congress of the United States voted that for one year members wear a black band on their sleeves in memory of the man who had led the American colonists in achieving Independence.

Bibliography

Adams, James Truslow. *The Adams Family.* Boston: Little, Brown & Co., 1930.

Adams, John. *The Adams Papers: Diary and Autobiography of John Adams.* Vol. I. New York: Atheneum, 1964.

Adams, John. "James Otis, Samuel Adams, and John Hancock: John Adams's Tributes to These as the Three Principal Movers and Agents of the American Revolution," *Old South Leaflets,* No. 179, 1817. Microfilm, New York Public Library.

Beach, Stewart. *Samuel Adams.* New York: Dodd, Mead & Co., 1965.

Billias, George Athan, editor. *George Washington's Opponents: British Generals and Admirals in the American Revolution.* New York: William Morrow & Co., 1969.

Bowen, Catherine Drinker. *The Miracle at Philadelphia: The Story of the Constitutional Convention.* Boston: Little, Brown & Co., 1966.

Brodie, Fawn M. *Thomas Jefferson: An Intimate History.* New York: W. W. Norton & Co., 1974.

Brown, Richard D. *Revolutionary Politics in Massachusetts: The Boston Committee of Correspondence and the Towns, 1772–1774.* Cambridge, Mass.: Harvard University Press, 1970.

Bruce, H. Addington. *Woman in the Making of America.* Boston: Little, Brown & Co., 1912.

Chastellux, Marquis de. *Travels in North America in the Years 1780, 1781 and 1782.* Vols. I and II. A revised translation with introduction and notes by Howard C. Rice, Jr. Chapel Hill, N.C.: The University of North Carolina Press, 1963.

Chidsey, Donald Barr. *The Loyalists: The Story of Those Americans Who Fought Against Independence.* New York: Crown, 1973.

Commager, Henry Steele, and Morris, Richard B. *The Spirit of 'Seventy-Six.* New York: Harper & Row, 1967.

Dupuy, R. Ernest, and Dupuy, Trevor N. *An Outline History of the American Revolution.* New York: Harper & Row, 1975.

Ellet, Elizabeth Fries. *Domestic History of the American Revolution.* New York: Baker and Scribner, 1850.

Encyclopaedia Britannica. 1953.

Fisher, Sydney George. *The True History of the American Revolution.* Philadelphia: J. B. Lippincott Co., 1902.

Fiske, John. *The American Revolution.* Vol. I. Boston: Houghton, Mifflin Co., 1896.

Flexner, James Thomas. *George Washington in the American Revolution.* Boston: Little, Brown & Co., 1967.

Forbes, Esther. *Paul Revere and the World He Lived In.* Boston: Houghton, Mifflin Co., 1942.

French, Allen. *General Gage's Informers.* Ann Arbor, Mich.: University of Michigan Press, 1932.

———. *The Siege of Boston.* New York: Macmillan Co., 1911.

Garraty, John A. *The American Nation.* New York: Harper & Row, 1966.

Garraty, John A., and Sternstein, Jerome L., editors. *The Harper Encyclopedia of American Biography.* New York: Harper & Row, 1974.

Harlow, Ralph Volney. *Samuel Adams.* New York: Henry Holt & Co., 1923.

Hosmer, James K. *Samuel Adams.* Boston: Houghton, Mifflin Co., 1885.

Jameson, J. Franklin (Director of Historical Research in the Carnegie Institution of Washington). *The American Revolution Considered as a Social Movement.* Princeton: Princeton University Press, 1926.

Jones, Howard Mumford, and Jones, Bessie Zaban, editors. *The Many Views of Boston.* Boston: An Atlantic Monthly Press Book, Little, Brown & Co., 1975.

Leckie, Robert. *The Wars of America.* New York: Harper & Row, 1968.

Leonard, Eugenia A.; Drinker, Sophie; and Holden, Miriam Y. *The American Woman in Colonial and Revolutionary Times: 1565–1800.* A Syllabus with Bibliography. Philadelphia: University of Pennsylvania Press, 1962.

Malone, Dumas. *The Story of the Declaration of Independence.* New York: Oxford University Press, 1954.

Miller, John C. *Sam Adams: Pioneer in Propaganda.* Boston: Little, Brown & Co., 1936.

Mitchell, Broadus. *The Price of Independence.* New York: Oxford University Press, 1974.

Montross, Lynn. *The Reluctant Rebels.* New York: Harper & Brothers, 1950.

Morison, Samuel Eliot. *The Growth of the American Republic.* New York: Oxford University Press, 1962.

_____. *The Oxford History of the American People.* New York: Oxford University Press, 1965.

Morris, Richard B., editor. *Encyclopedia of American History.* New York: Harper & Row, 1965.

_____. *Seven Who Shaped Our Destiny.* New York: Harper & Row, 1973.

_____. *The American Revolution Reconsidered.* New York: Harper & Row, 1967.

Peabody, James Bishop, editor. *John Adams: A Biography in His Own Words.* The Founding Fathers Series. New York: Harper & Row, 1973.

Pearson, Michael. *Those Damned Rebels: The American Revolution as Seen Through British Eyes.* New York: G. P. Putnam's Sons, 1972.

Richards, Laura. *Abigail Adams and Her Times.* New York: D. Appleton and Co., 1917.

Schlesinger, Arthur M. *The Birth of the Nation: A Portrait of the American People on the Eve of Independence.* New York: Alfred A. Knopf, 1968.

Shipton, Clifford K. *Sibley's Harvard Graduates.* Vol. X. Boston: Massachusetts Historical Society, 1958.

Tourtellot, Arthur B. *William Diamond's Drum.* New York: Doubleday & Co., 1959.

Trevelyan, George Otto. *The American Revolution.* New York: David McKay Co., 1964.

Wecter, Dixon. *The Hero in America.* New York: Charles Scribner's Sons, 1941.

Wells, H. G. *The Outline of History.* New York: Macmillan Co., 1920.

Wells, William V. *The Life and Public Services of Samuel Adams.* Vol. I. Books for Libraries Press, 1969. Originally published in 1865.

Winston, Alexander. "Firebrand of the Revolution." *American Heritage,* April 1967.

Zobel, Hiller B. *The Boston Massacre.* New York: W. W. Norton & Co., 1970.

Index

James Otis

George R. III

G. Washington

John Hancock

Israel Putnam

B. Arnold